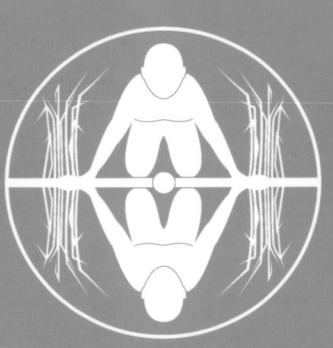

A POWERFUL TOOL TO ENHANCE YOUR RELATIONSHIP

GEOFF CHARLEY & LUCY LIDELL

THE MIRROR CARDS

About the Authors

LUCY LIDELL is co-author of the international bestseller *The New Book of Massage* and *The New Book of Yoga*, and author of *The Sensual Body*. For the past twenty years, her main sphere of interest has been in healing therapies and spiritual transformation. She now runs a private massage and healing practice and leads workshops in meditation and self-development.

GEOFF CHARLEY worked for twenty five years in advertising and marketing. He was Creative and Technical Director of a design and production company, and a director of a large international advertising agency. His interest in psychology, philosophy and alternative thinking led him to explore numerous therapies and to train in Transpersonal Psychotherapy. He now writes fiction and non-fiction and has a private psychotherapy and counselling practice in Hampshire.

Visit The Mirror Cards website at
www.themirrorcards.com
and let us know your comments on the pack.

THE
MIRROR CARDS

A POWERFUL TOOL TO ENHANCE YOUR RELATIONSHIP

GEOFF CHARLEY & LUCY LIDELL

Mandala images by Oliver Burston

A CONNECTIONS EDITION
This edition published in Great Britain in 2003 by
Connections Book Publishing Limited
St Chad's House, 148 King's Cross Road, London WC1X 9DH

This edition published in the USA in 2003 by
Connections Book Publishing Limited.
Distributed in the USA by RedWheel/Weiser,
368 Congress Street, Boston, MA 02210

Text copyright © Geoff Charley & Lucy Lidell 2003
Mandala images copyright © Oliver Burston 2003
This edition copyright © Eddison Sadd Editions 2003

All rights reserved. No part of this book may be reproduced,
stored in a retrieval system, or transmitted in any form or by any means without
the prior written permission of the publisher, nor be otherwise circulated in any
form of binding or cover other than that in which it is published and without
a similar condition being imposed on the subsequent purchaser.

British Library Cataloguing-in-Publication data available on request.

ISBN 1-85906-132-X

1 3 5 7 9 10 8 6 4 2

Phototypeset in Giovanni and Futura using QuarkXPress
on Apple Macintosh

Origination by Modern Age Repro House Ltd, Hong Kong
Printed in China by Hung Hing

CONTENTS

INTRODUCTION	6	QUESTIONS AND ANSWERS	17
HOW TO USE THE CARDS	11	THE PACK IN PRACTICE	21

THE CARDS   27

1	ACCEPTANCE	28	17	INITIATING	102
2	ACTION	33	18	INTEGRITY	107
3	ALONENESS	38	19	JOY	112
4	ANGER	43	20	LETTING GO	117
5	APPRECIATION	49	21	NURTURE	122
6	BOUNDARIES	54	22	OBJECTIVITY	126
7	CHANGE	59	23	REALITY	131
8	CHOICE	63	24	RESPONSIBILITY	136
9	COMMUNICATION	67	25	SADNESS	141
10	EMPATHY	71	26	SELF-WORTH	146
11	EXPRESSION	75	27	SEXUALITY	151
12	FREEDOM	79	28	SPONTANEITY	157
13	FRIENDSHIP	84	29	TRUST	161
14	HONESTY	89	30	VULNERABILITY	166
15	HUMOUR	93	31	WILL	170
16	INDEPENDENCE	98	32	THE MIRROR	174

FURTHER READING AND ACKNOWLEDGEMENTS   176

INTRODUCTION

THE MIRROR CARDS PROVIDE a simple, accurate means of pinpointing and working with relationship difficulties. The power of the pack lies in its ability to connect you, through your own unconscious, to the synchronous choice of a card, so that if you are genuinely seeking a solution to your problems you have a unique set of tools at hand to help you.

The cards are based on 'mirroring' – the principle that the world reflects back to you what you most need to learn. You attract to yourself exactly the right people, at the right time, for the right lesson. But it is your choice whether to take the opportunity to learn, or not.

THE GIFT OF RELATIONSHIP

WHEN A POWERFUL ATTRACTION first draws two people together, many of the reasons for the attraction are unconscious. Yet each partner, to some extent, represents the potential of the other. There may be obvious differences from which each can learn. Perhaps one is gregarious, the other something of a loner, so each has an opportunity to investigate the opposite aspect in themselves. But the greatest gifts can be far subtler than this.

It is in the rawness of our feelings that the greatest gifts lie, whether it be in the open-heartedness of love, the hot rage of hatred, or the emptiness of abandonment. It isn't a mistake that we feel these things. It's what we draw to ourselves in order to learn. And each of these feelings will be 'mirroring' some part of ourselves that needs attention so that we can learn, and grow.

If we choose not to pay attention to the parts of ourselves that are mirrored, we continue to follow one of two patterns. Either we stay in a long-term relationship, feeling stuck in a recurring cycle of behaviour, or we keep starting new relationships that at first seem better or different from the last one, but which end up mirroring back to us the same problems. In both patterns, we will probably blame our partners for our unhappiness.

What is needed is for us to recognize and receive these gifts, if we are not to feel disappointed once the initial romance begins to fade.

This pack offers you a way out of both these patterns. It will show that you are much more powerful than you ever imagined, that you create your own reality, and that no matter how good or bad you believe your relationship to be, you are being presented with an opportunity to really see the truth of yourself.

The Mirror Cards will enable you to discover the gifts your partner is offering you, whatever form they take. They will help you to confront and change those aspects of yourself that obstruct the flow of love and intimacy, and support the positive aspects that you have already developed. For change can only come through awareness. After all, how can you change what you're doing until you *know* what you're doing?

A healthy relationship has a life of its own. In the same way that we all fluctuate in feelings from day to day, so does a relationship. In the same way that we all feel low from time to time, so does a relationship. There is a natural ebb and flow, and consequently no possibility of a perfect balance. The richness of a relationship lies in its ever-changing nature and the challenges those changes bring.

Expecting your relationship to be a never-ending source of love and comfort places a huge burden on it. But neither should you resign yourself to it remaining stuck in a dark mire. Sometimes you will need to allow the relationship to do its work without interference, and at other times you will need to engage with it.

Through using the cards this changing nature of relationships will be brought sharply into focus, helping you to decide when to work on your relationship and when to just let it be.

THE MIRROR CARDS

By putting you in touch with your own deeper awareness, the cards aim to clarify what particular issue you need to look at right now. They are not designed to predict your future, nor to tell you what is happening in your relationship as a whole, since any card you draw only relates to your part of the dynamic.

Used consistently, the cards will help you to keep re-focusing on behaviour that undermines you and support you in making permanent changes. They can help you to come to terms with your all-too-human weaknesses and fears, strengthening you in who you are, rather than who you think you should be.

You may be given advice at times that you do not want to hear. If you do feel resistant to it, bear in mind that the guidance contained in the cards is simply an extension of your own wisdom.

We often reject our own wisdom, as it can challenge us to turn our belief systems, or even our lives, upside down. The value of using the cards is that you have absolute, conscious control as to whether you choose to heed them or not. You can applaud their wisdom as your own, or dismiss it. The choice is yours. But it is our hope that the cards will gradually lead you to listen to and trust your own inner knowing, so that one day you will no longer have need of them.

We sincerely extend our best wishes to you and honour your intention to take responsibility for yourself and your relationship. It is only through the path of individual self-awareness that the world can genuinely change for the better.

HOW TO USE THE CARDS

Y̲OU WILL GAIN the most from a card reading if you treat the whole process with respect and prepare yourself before making a selection. We strongly suggest that you follow the simple steps outlined here, each time you take a card. It will not only help you to focus on the issue but also to receive the most benefit from the answer.

1. MAKE SURE YOU ARE ON YOUR OWN.

The presence of any other person, in particular someone with whom you are in relationship, will have an effect on you and therefore influence the card you draw. Whenever there are two or more people together, powerful, unconscious energies are at work – sometimes helpful, sometimes disruptive. In an ideal world, you would be strong enough not to be affected, but given the subject matter you are dealing with, it is important to minimize external influences.

2. SUMMARIZE THE ISSUE SO IT IS ABOUT YOURSELF.

Think about the issue you are faced with and try to reduce it to its essence. And make sure you ask about yourself, not your partner. For example, if you are wondering whether to end the relationship because you can't stand your partner's jealous behaviour, the issue is not about your partner doing something: it's about your reaction to it. So the problem becomes either: 'The issue is my wanting to leave the relationship' or 'The issue is my reaction to my partner's jealousy.' You could draw a card for each one.

Notice if you find it hard to phrase the issue around yourself. If you do, this indicates a tendency on your part to avoid taking responsibility, which is very common. Don't feel bad about it; be pleased that you are starting to see it!

3. PHRASE YOUR ISSUE AS A STATEMENT.

Rather than asking a direct question, such as: 'Why am I feeling so hurt?', it is better to formulate your problem as a statement: 'The issue is my feeling hurt.'

4. RELAX! BREATHE OUT! LET GO!

The intention behind the cards is to connect you with the calm, wise part of yourself – the part that can provide you with helpful and objective advice. To facilitate that connection, you need to begin by letting go of any emotions you are holding in your body. Check your body for tension, especially your head, neck, shoulders and stomach. Relax those muscles! Let go of all those emotions! Take a few slow deep breaths, extending the out-breath, and let go of the belief that you know what the answer will be.

5. CLOSE YOUR EYES …

Hold the issue very clearly in your mind while you shuffle the cards.

6. OPEN YOUR EYES …

Spread the cards out in front of you face down. Create a 'chaos' of cards. Muddle them about as much as you like. The cards as a whole represent the chaos of the issue. While you are spreading them out, keep your eyes focused on the image on the backs of the cards, especially the dot in the centre of the circle, as this symbolizes the self.

7. CHOOSE A CARD – ANY CARD!

Make sure the card is in a vertical position before you turn it over. Keep it in the position in which you have turned it over, whether it's the right way up, so the number and name can be read, or upside down. If it is Inverse (upside down), leave it that way.

8. TURN TO THE READING.

Using the number on the card to help you find the reading, refer to the book for a deeper understanding of the issue. The card texts appear alphabetically in the book, except for THE MIRROR card, which comes last.

The introductions to each card embody the core of the issue you are facing – the essential truth. What follows contains guidance on what is being reflected back to you in 'choosing' the card at this particular moment.

Read the text slowly, especially if it's a card you have chosen before. You may find a different emphasis in the interpretation each time you read it.

9. NOTICE WHAT YOU FEEL.

Do you welcome, or want to reject, this card? Do you recognize yourself in it? The more you can stay with whatever feelings or understandings are brought up for you by the text, the more you will gain from it.

If you find the guidance hard to accept, just hang a question mark over your head for a while. Be open to the possibilities before totally rejecting them. Often the greatest truths about ourselves are the most difficult to accept, triggering strong reactions. Yet they also provide wonderful opportunities for change – if only we can find the courage to work with them.

You may choose a card that simply echoes what you are already doing. If this happens, don't make the mistake of assuming it's wrong. Stay with what you're doing, even if it's difficult.

10. ACT ON THE READING AT ONCE.

Hesitation and delay will only weaken your resolve and dilute the potency of the information you have received.

QUICK REFERENCE SUMMARY

1. Make sure you are on your own.
2. Summarize the issue so it is about yourself.
3. Phrase your issue as a statement.
4. Relax! Breathe out! Let go!
5. Close your eyes. Hold the issue very clearly in your mind while you shuffle the cards.
6. Open your eyes. Spread the cards out in front of you.
7. Choose a card – any card!
8. Turn to the reading.
9. Notice what you feel.
10. Act on the reading at once.

QUESTIONS AND ANSWERS

When should I use the cards?
You can use the cards at any time to gain insight on an issue, but their objective viewpoint will be especially helpful whenever you are feeling puzzled or upset in your relationship. At such times, your own powerful emotions may prevent you from seeing what is really happening, and it is easy then to fall into the trap of blaming your partner for 'making you feel bad'.

Consulting the cards and seeing what is being mirrored back to you at moments like these can prove very revealing, and enable you to take responsibility for what you are eliciting from your partner, rather than feeling like a victim. You may also recognize a familiar pattern in your way of being, and start to understand more about the dynamics between the two of you.

What does Inverse mean?
All the card texts end with the Inverse reading, which you should refer to if you turned the card over with the word and number upside down.

The Inverse is not necessarily the opposite of the upright card. It reflects the same issue, but in distorted form – the dynamic has become exaggerated. For example, the upright text for BOUNDARIES hinges on the need to know your limits and develop self-protection, while the Inverse reflects a tendency to be prickly and defensive.

If you find that you repeatedly draw inverted cards, your core issue may be resistance or defensiveness. Recognizing such a pattern is the first step to changing it.

What does it mean if I keep picking up the same card in answer to different issues?
This is not magic. It's what you need to look at, not only in your relationship but also, most probably, in other areas of your life. It is a core issue and can show you the root belief or relationship pattern that is undermining you. Pay attention, for it will continue to crop up if you don't deal with it!

How will identifying my core issues help me?
Awareness is everything. Once you can see what you're doing, you can choose to continue that behaviour or to do something else. And if you find yourself struggling to change the way you relate, seek the support of an experienced counsellor or therapist, or arrange regular meetings with a group of friends who also want to change the way they relate. There is great value in sharing your feelings and discovering you're not the only one struggling.

Can I draw more than one card?
Yes, but only if you sincerely wish to deepen your understanding of the first card.

How often can I draw cards?
There is no limit, but watch out for any tendency to rely on them for all your answers. The Mirror Cards are intended to strengthen your awareness, not to take its place. Their effectiveness is linked to your own focus and seriousness of intention. Drawing two or three cards a day, for example, would indicate dependence or a tendency for your mind to be scattered rather than focused.

Can I consult the cards about past relationships?
Yes. It can be rewarding to draw a card to gain insight on issues you were confronting with a past lover. Learning more about the patterns you encountered in your relationships in the past can stop you repeating the same lessons with your present partner. But avoid tuning in to more than one relationship at one sitting.

Can I draw cards for problems with family or friends?
The Mirror Cards are primarily intended to help you steer your way more consciously through intimate relationship problems, but you can also use them to clarify an issue between yourself and someone you are close to. After all, what is being reflected is always about yourself.

Should I focus on the symbolic nature of the card images?
No. The beautiful images simply support the text, reflecting the changing nature of our rich internal worlds. But they may well stimulate your own thoughts and beliefs about the issue concerned.

THE PACK IN PRACTICE

To give you an idea of how you can work with the cards, we have included three first-hand accounts from people who have been using the pack over a period of a few months.

First, Jo, a self-aware woman in her mid-twenties who is using The Mirror Cards to negotiate the ups and downs of her relationship.

The first time Jo used the pack was when Michael had gone away for the weekend. He'd said that he would be back on Sunday afternoon and would call to arrange an evening together …

'I waited, but Michael didn't call until after 8 o'clock. When we spoke I got angry and said that it was too late to arrange anything. I came off the phone, upset at his lack of consideration and my anger turned to tears. I looked to The Mirror Cards for some understanding of what was happening.

'I drew INITIATING. Reading the text, I realized that the card was reflecting my general passivity in life, and it reminded me of the familiar scenario of sitting and waiting for a man to call me whenever he felt like it. The card suggested I look at what was stopping me taking up the reins a little more myself. I knew there was truth in this – I seemed to always hand over to Michael the responsibility for our dates because I didn't want him to think I was controlling.'

So rather than carry on being angry with Michael – justified though it may have been! – Jo had an opportunity to understand what the situation was reflecting about herself. But she also felt annoyed that she was so upset, feeling that it was weak to cry over something so seemingly trivial. She wanted to know more about her tendency to cry in such situations, so she took another card.

'This time I drew SADNESS, which encouraged me to allow the feelings I was having. It was interesting, too, because it reflected that when a reaction seems out of proportion to the event, it may be because we are subconsciously being reminded of past experiences. In my case, I realized that I was always waiting for my father to pay attention to me – to love me and acknowledge my feelings. He never did. And now I was having the same experience mirrored to me through Michael.'

Through the SADNESS card, Jo was being shown how important it was for her not to judge her tears but to release the feelings that she had suppressed from childhood.

NICK IS THIRTY-FIVE and has had a number of long-term relationships. He wanted a dependable partner with whom he could have children. He and his present partner, Sophie, had been together for two years, but he felt they were 'not good for each other' and wanted to finish the relationship. He phrased his issue as: 'My wanting to end the relationship'.

'I drew the FREEDOM card, inverted, which indicated that perhaps I would be running away if I finished with Sophie. I really felt this card was completely wrong since I believed that I'd done everything possible to make the relationship work. So I reshuffled and drew again – and got the same card, FREEDOM, inverted!

Angry, I drew again, and this time it was THE MIRROR, reflecting that I knew all I needed to know.'

In talking through this and many similar experiences he had with the cards, we discovered that it was extremely hard for Nick to view himself objectively. He firmly believed that he was doing all he could and that ultimately the problem was his partner's. Although he persisted in seeking support through the cards, whenever his beliefs were challenged, he would reject the card he drew in his desire to be 'right'.

Nick reflects perfectly how we can only hear what we are ready to hear. Our attachments to our beliefs can blind us to the truth, even though the truth can set us free. So, stay open to the card you choose even if you feel it is utterly wrong.

In Nick's case we were able to challenge his block and he successfully moved through it. At times, you too may find it helpful to supplement your use of The Mirror Cards by working with an experienced psychotherapist or counsellor.

SARA IS FORTY, married with two young children and in a business partnership with her husband.

Having seen some of the book texts, Sara asked for a pack of The Mirror Cards and went on to use it in an unusual way. She was in a very happy and supportive marriage but wanted to use the cards to investigate her problems with family and friends. After seven weeks, she reported that she was undergoing profound life changes.

'The cards helped me to understand my desire to please and appease others, particularly my domineering father. The SELF-WORTH card came up a number of times and through it I learned to start valuing myself and my actions – and to stand my ground with my father without entering into conflict with him. As a bonus, I found I could successfully diet for the first time in my life, managing to lose the weight I gained after my second child. Also, once I'd understood many of the dynamics at play within my friendships, I was able to start re-evaluating who my friends really were.'

As we discussed her experiences with her, it became clear that it was her desire to change, partnered with the support of the pack, that had caused a transformation in her that was dramatic enough for others to notice and comment on. Not only was Sara using the cards to deal with issues when they arose, she was reading texts at random with no intention other than to muse on their content and relevance to her.

It is often said that there is no change without the desire to do so. Sara used the pack in her own way as a tool for change. If, for you, it means reading one of the texts each day, or tearing out pages and pinning them to the wall, or taping a card to your dashboard, do it! Throw away the rules, including ours, and reach out with passion for what you need.

THE CARDS

The world is reflecting back to you who you are.

*In every moment you have a choice
as to how you see it.*

*Begin to make new choices
and the world will begin to change.*

It's that simple.

1

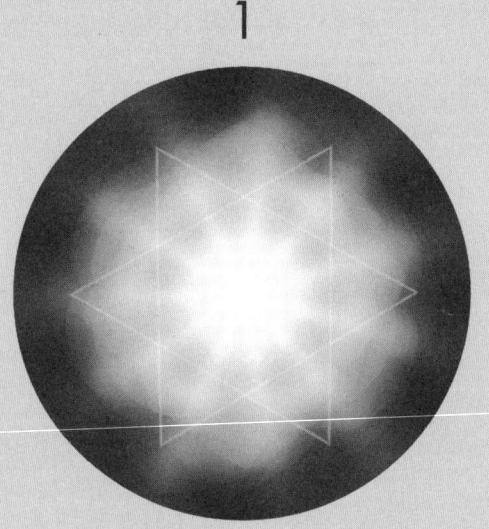

ACCEPTANCE

It's a great relief when you accept the way it is, even if it's not very nice; because the only real misery is not wanting it to be like that.

AJAHN SUMEDHO

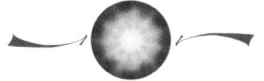

*Acceptance is the ending of the struggle
to change or deny the way things are –
even though there may be a desire
for them to be different.*

YOU SEEM TO BE HOLDING ON to an image of how you want someone or something to be. You have a dream – or a plan. But what you want is clearly not happening. And even though it's not, you're still trying to force it.

Whatever your situation, you are being asked to just accept things the way they are – and this may not be at all easy for you.

You are probably feeling dissatisfaction, even antagonism, wanting to fight or protest loudly. But it is your lack of acceptance that is causing much of your discomfort, rather than the situation itself.

If you are having critical thoughts, finding it hard to accept someone as they are, consider the possibility that this is a reflection of your own self-criticism, of your difficulty in accepting yourself. If you can't fully accept the way you are, you won't be able to accept someone else.

The way through is first to acknowledge and then accept all of the feelings and reactions you are having, without inhibition or judgement.

If you find the concept of acceptance hard to believe in, or associate it with weakness, consider the word a little more deeply. It means giving up resistance, not giving *up*, and allowing life to provide what it is that you need.

We often struggle to give ourselves one thing, while life, in its wisdom, is trying to give us something else. But we cannot always understand what is happening or where our life path is going. Sometimes we just have to follow it.

Do not underestimate the power of acceptance. This is an extremely potent card that indicates the possibility of immense, positive change – if only you will allow it.

Give up the struggle. Go with the flow of events that

is naturally taking place. Life could in fact be *offering* you something here.

INVERSE

Where acceptance involves a conscious surrendering to the reality of things, resignation is giving up on what we want out of a sense of defeat – and the belief that we can't have it anyway.

YOU APPEAR TO BE under the misapprehension that you've just got to put up with the situation as it is and suffer in silence. But there's a world of difference between healthy acceptance and hopeless apathy.

Have you decided that you don't have the power to choose in this situation? Have you handed over your authority to someone else? Perhaps you've chosen martyrdom, or just peace at any price.

If you're tired of stoically tolerating others' behaviour, putting up with scraps in case there's nothing more, it's time to take your seat at the table, instead of waiting mournfully beneath it.

As long as you act like an underdog, obediently lying down when you're told to, people will treat you that way. And really, who can blame them?

Get out of that dog basket! Bark. Snarl. Growl. Have the courage of your convictions and dare to stand up for yourself. You'll discover that your thoughts and feelings are just as valid as anyone else's.

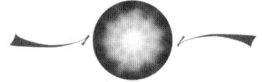

2

ACTION

*Action may not always bring happiness,
but there is no happiness without action.*

BENJAMIN DISRAELI

To take action is to initiate change.
To take action is to use your power.
To take action is to be creative and bold.

People who complain of not being creative tend not to act – they 're-act' to others or situations. They wait until decisions are taken out of their hands.

Action involves moving an idea out of the realms of thought into physical reality. Without action, thoughts and ideas remain sterile, gathering dust like unread books on a shelf, and energy stagnates, supporting a belief of personal powerlessness.

You can plan and ponder, reaching endless wise realizations, but unless you put your thoughts into action, nothing will actually move. The time for action is now.

You've probably mastered the art of procrastination – postponing things until the right time, waiting for someone else to decide matters, even for destiny to intervene. But you have sat back long enough.

By not acting, you are not taking part in the play of life. In Shakespeare's words: 'All the world's a stage. And all the men and women merely players.' But are you taking your place on stage? Or are you still waiting in the wings, rehearsing your lines?

In your 'non-action' there may be fear – perhaps not knowing which way to go, not wanting to get it wrong, being concerned for the repercussions. You may have a sense of paralysis, like a rabbit caught in headlights. But there are no guarantees of safety in life, and you have to be prepared to make mistakes in order to move forward.

Whatever you decide to do, take your courage in both hands and stay with your decision, no matter how uncomfortable it feels. Like flexing a little-used muscle, it may ache. There may even be a feeling of loss as you move from the safe zone of inactivity.

Only when you are well into the course of action you have settled on should you review the situation and decide whether it still feels appropriate, despite your discomfort and fear.

Just by moving from that dormant and passive place you are gaining power, and any hesitancy or inertia will evaporate, to be replaced by a feeling of empowerment and a sense of your own authority. *Trust* yourself.

INVERSE

Overactivity is a sure sign that something is being avoided. It is not always through doing that the most important things get done.

ACTION CREATES CHANGE, but perhaps you're moving on before you have had a chance to fully be with what is happening in the present. Like the tourist who leaps from the car, snaps a photo and zooms off to the next sight, you could be missing out, skimming the surface and tiring yourself and others with your frenetic activity.

Turn the engine off, put the camera down and take a long, slow walk through the situation as it is. Drawing this card inverted is telling you to spend time 'being' rather than 'doing'. So relax, and breathe it all in.

There may be something here that is hard for you to face. Do you believe deep down that relationships should be smooth and easy, and if they're anything else they're not working? Do you get bored easily and move on? Is it hard for you to just laze around with your partner without feeling agitated?

Notice if what you are doing is just a reaction to the discomfort of the situation. Check carefully to see if you are avoiding something, maybe from fear of allowing someone to get too close. Then wonder if that's the way you always want it to be …

3

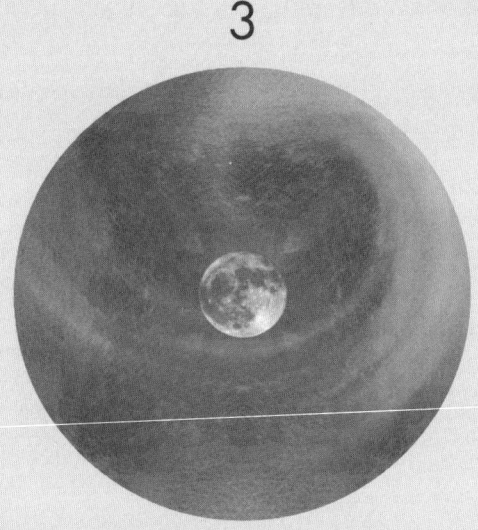

ALONENESS

To be alone is like being with a friend whose company will last forever.

JOHANN WOLFGANG VON GOETHE

Aloneness is the experience of profound inner fullness and wholeness – a state of 'all-oneness' that springs from a deep sense of connection.

YOU ARE FACED WITH SEEING through the illusion of the sad, lonely figure wandering along the beach, lost and broken-hearted, and challenged to find true strength within yourself, *not* through the solace of a relationship.

Your task is to find the time and space to be with yourself, away from the confusions that surround you. If you spend too much time in others' company, you risk losing touch with your own deeper needs and feelings.

We all have endless strategies for avoiding the feeling of solitude – keeping ourselves busy, socializing when our heart isn't in it, compulsively seeking a new partner to fill the void as soon as we are not in a relationship. But sooner or later we have to face ourselves and find our sense of security from within, *not* through other people.

Aloneness is not loneliness. While loneliness brings feelings of emptiness and self-pity and a distancing from everything and everyone, aloneness connects you with the essence of life that runs through all things, empowering you through the knowledge that you are never alone.

Any experience that connects you with the present moment would be helpful. You could try staying at home more, with the TV and telephone turned off. Lie in the bath, just enjoying the physical sensation, letting go of the events of the day. Watch a candle flicker, a tree waving in the wind or sunlight on the floor. Start writing a daily log, not just of what you did, but of your deepest thoughts and feelings, whatever they are.

Above all, take the opportunity to follow your heart and seek the things that strengthen and nourish you.

If you are feeling lonely even though you have a partner, you are touching an important truth about relationships – you cannot expect your partner to fill your emptiness. That deep ache in your heart has a purpose: to drive you to look inside, instead of searching for validation outside.

Discovering the essence of aloneness takes some time. You will not do it in one evening, and you may find that you pass through states of deep loneliness along the way. Allow any pain that you may have been avoiding to come forward, but always remember your intention – to uncover the strength that lies within your vulnerability. For to feel all things is to know all-oneness.

INVERSE

Isolation is not our natural way of being. It is a place we go to, either from fear or hopelessness.

YOU SEEM TO HAVE FORGOTTEN that 'no man is an island' and have cut yourself off from the nourishment and companionship others can provide. Consciously or unconsciously, you are avoiding intimacy, perhaps because at some time in your life you took in the message 'love hurts'. But if you don't take the risk of allowing someone to get close to you, you will never be able to heal this belief.

Dare to reach out of your protective cocoon, and try letting people in, too. Don't wait for someone else to make the first move. Others may not realize that you feel shy or isolated, for you may give the impression of being self-sufficient, even proud. If you would only ask, they might be able to support you in stepping into the stream of life.

Let others know you feel vulnerable, but have the courage to meet them halfway. Remember, it's not only you who is afraid.

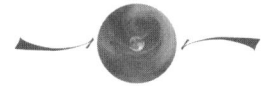

4

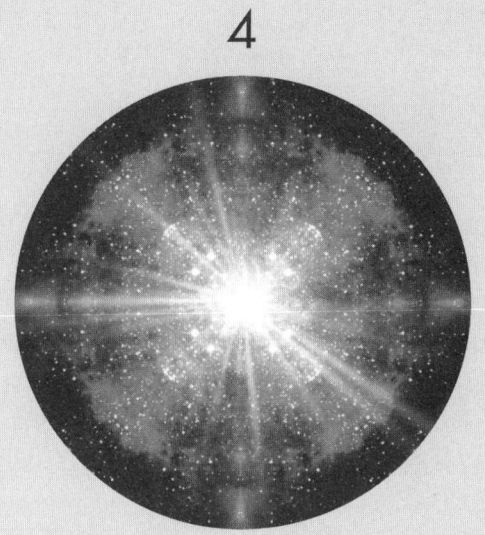

ANGER

*Better a moment of anger,
than a lifetime of resentment.*

PAULA REBUCK

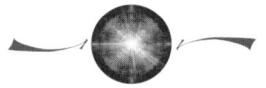

*Anger can be constructive
as well as destructive.
It can be the fire that cleanses away the old,
making space for the new.
Or it can be the fire that just destroys.
It can be the hand that is raised to say 'Stop!'
Or it can be the hand that strikes.*

YOU MAY BE HARBOURING resentment and using indirect ways of expressing your anger – through sarcasm, sulking, playing the martyr, or withdrawing. Perhaps you're even acting very happy, as if to say 'Look how not angry I am!'

You may not recognize that what you are feeling is, in fact, anger and believe it to be disappointment or hurt. So you may be surprised at getting this card. Maybe you find those feelings more acceptable, and are using them as a cover for your anger.

Some of us are so convinced that anger is wrong

that we manage to persuade ourselves that we *have* no anger. But when anger is denied it either leaks out in passive–aggressive behaviour or builds up, eventually bursting out in explosive rages. If there is no outlet at all, it can even make us ill.

Anger itself is not the problem. How we use it, can be. This card suggests that the anger you are experiencing is appropriate, and in your situation you may need to consider doing something with it.

But first, identify what is blocking your anger. What are you concerned will happen if you say how angry you really are? That you will hurt someone? That someone else will become angry and perhaps leave? That you will be seen as bad, or unreasonable, or inconsiderate of others' feelings?

Recognize that these are all avoidance strategies and see how your lack of expression actually comes from fear. That fear is of losing control – of yourself, of the other person, of the situation. And the fear is that of a child, not an adult. Maturity brings the ability to express feelings of anger, while holding back the destructive elements.

The best way to honour anger is to state what you feel cleanly, either at the time or as soon as possible after the event. To say 'I am really angry!' without lashing out. To simply express what you are experiencing without the need to blame or manipulate the other person. To let go of controlling.

Sometimes our anger *is* selfish, lacking in either logic or an understanding of the other party, but that doesn't mean we should suppress it. Just saying 'I am so angry!' can lead to a letting go of something that otherwise lurks in the shadows – an avenging monster waiting for its opportunity. It can also lead to a clearing of the air and therefore bring you and your partner closer together, as you reveal more of who you are. You don't have to get it right all the time!

Recognize that anger is essential: to defend our boundaries; to stop manipulation; to protect ourselves against hurtful, demeaning and even dangerous behaviour; to maintain our personal power.

It is better to say 'No!' at the wrong time, than not to say it at all.

INVERSE

Anger that is directed towards people in order to hurt them or make them change is abuse.

YOUR FEELINGS ARE VERY STRONG and you sense that you are losing control. You want to show how much you are hurting, but your tendency is to get into a rage.

The line between expressing anger appropriately and being abusive is quite clear, and you are in danger of crossing that line. Realizing this can be difficult, if flying into a rage has always been your way of expressing anger. You can only see what you're doing by pulling back to an objective position, which is probably the last place you want to be!

You are entitled to whatever feelings you have and it is important to show them. But it's also important not to inflict them on others. Let them know what you are feeling – then leave them space to respond. Let them decide for themselves what their reaction is, without having to fear an onslaught from you.

Attacking someone may make you feel powerful,

but that sense of power is a false one, and behind it cowers a profound feeling of powerlessness.

Take the words of blame out of what you say. Remove threats. Don't belittle, intimidate, attack or provoke. Simply describe your feeling of anger and what you feel is happening. No-one is doing anything *to* you – this is just how you are experiencing the situation. Someone else in your situation might experience it entirely differently.

A useful technique is to imagine a table between you and the person you are angry with. Rather than dumping your anger on the other person, dump all your anger on the table, where you can both see it. It's like emptying your pockets or your bag to see what you have in there. It takes you to a clearer vantage point. And it can provide a space in which to understand, in a deeper way, why your anger is so aggressive. You will also find that the table provides a safe 'container' for your feelings instead of you 'punching air' and the dissatisfaction that brings.

5

APPRECIATION

*Have the eyes of a child
and the heart of a lover.*

Appreciation is the heart-felt state of seeing and welcoming all that is positive in our lives.

WE OFTEN FAIL to appreciate something just because it's ours. What we have can seem worthless, while what we don't have appears far more desirable.

Lack of appreciation comes from measuring our lives against one of the great illusions. The 'dream-makers' don't want us to appreciate what we have. They want us to feel dissatisfied so we'll change it for something better, newer, smarter. They depend on the fact that we would rather live in the future and avoid staying in the present.

As long as we are always looking to the next rush of adrenaline – the new toy, the new clothes, the new relationship – we can never be at peace. Happiness and contentment can only be found in the now. It's impossible to find them by looking to the future or reminiscing on what might have been.

So how can you begin to appreciate what you have? By seeing what it feels like to embrace with your heart everything that you are now questioning.

When did you last mentally list all the good things in your relationship? How often do you compliment your partner, and how often criticize? Everyone of your thoughts, words and actions serves to build your relationship, and they are *your* choices. They are the building blocks that make up the house of relationship you live in.

Wonderful relationships are not made in heaven. They take two people looking for the soul in one another. And hellish relationships take two people looking for the devil …

Notice the way society pays great attention to finding what is wrong with things, and very little to what is right. Look at how much more airtime is given to bad news than to good. There's a common, but strange belief that appreciation is somehow weak and that positive change comes only after criticism!

Have you fallen into this trap of negative perception? If so, beware! You're in danger of losing the ability to 'glow' with appreciation.

In appreciating someone you will be opening to closeness, and this will have repercussions. You may experience fear: of commitment, of having chosen the wrong person, of having lowered your guard. But you may also feel a depth of loving you have never before experienced.

This card is telling you to stop looking around, or ahead, or behind, and see what is right under your nose. Don't let this be a case of 'you don't know what you've got until it's gone'!

INVERSE

*Ingratiating ourselves is not appreciation.
It's surrendering our power – and ultimately
the control of the relationship.*

RATHER THAN BEING TRULY APPRECIATIVE of your partner's qualities, you seem to be in an 'ever so grateful, aren't I lucky?, thank you, thank you' place.

In fact this has nothing to do with how much you appreciate your partner, and everything to do with how little you think of yourself.

You may be displaying this tendency by giving your partner presents. This actually says more about your need to give than about what your partner wants to receive. Or perhaps you are behaving in a tremendously loving or admiring way.

Your partner may bask in the compliments for a while, but a pedestal is ultimately a very lonely place.

Self-deprecation and ingratiation are not the best foundations for a strong relationship, and neither will they strengthen you.

It's time to stop idealizing. Get your partner down off that pedestal – it's easier to see what's real when you're on the same level. Appreciate your own qualities and just be yourself. Either there's a great relationship waiting to happen founded on equality, or you'll discover you've been deluding yourself!

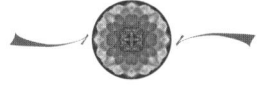

6

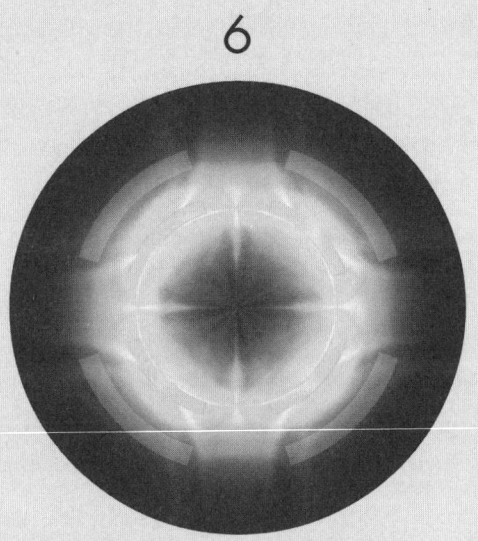

BOUNDARIES

Two are at one only when they remain two.

LOU ANDREAS-SALOME

Boundaries are the invisible borders that surround each one of us like a second skin. They make the container that we fill with who we are – our sense of self.

IT'S A COMMON FALLACY to believe that love means dropping our boundaries in order to be closer to our partners, and it's true that it *feels* like intimacy. But this is not the intimacy of an adult: it's the rekindling of the childhood need for love and safety, when pleasing someone else was the only way to feel close and loved.

Perhaps this false intimacy has led to you becoming a 'people-pleaser' – orbiting around the needs of your partner and allowing their emotions to invade you. Perhaps you're scared of stating your own needs for fear of causing conflict.

Boundaries are like our immune system. They support what is healthy and life-enhancing and resist what is not. So people with a good sense of boundaries recognize when they have had enough. They know their own limits and are able to shut the door and say 'No'.

Do you know what you want? Are you able to use your power of expression to draw the line? Can you truly distinguish what strengthens you from what weakens you? You are certainly being asked to question yourself now.

Holding strong, healthy boundaries enables us to say 'Yes' or 'No' at the right times; to let in people who can care for and support us, and to keep out people who may hurt us.

We need boundaries to retain a sense of ourselves as separate, autonomous beings when relating to others. Without them we find it hard to know who's doing what to whom. And in the confusion, we can find ourselves taken over and lose a sense of our own direction.

You may need to take some time out from your partner to do your own thing, or even to discover what your thing is! It may feel threatening at first – you may fear others leaving if you don't give them what they want. But if the relationship is to be real and enduring, it requires you to take time to increase your confidence.

A dynamic partnership is made up of two complete individuals who respect each other's boundaries.

Building healthy boundaries is not something you can do overnight. Changing a deep-seated pattern is confronting and takes time, awareness and *strength*. But if you're prepared to start now and to persevere, you will learn to stop giving yourself away and begin to forge a life that serves your very highest good.

INVERSE

When boundaries become walls, partners become enemies.

WHY ARE YOU FEELING the need to protect yourself so strongly? It seems you have become prickly and defensive, turning what might have been healthy boundaries into fortress walls, behind which you cannot be reached. Such entrenchment inevitably leads to isolation and a sense that your partner is the enemy. Is this really what you want?

Your armouring may not only be guarding you from

what's outside: it may also be preventing you from knowing what's going on inside. For when the focus of blame is on someone else, it's easier to ignore where your own responsibility lies.

Ask yourself whether some core belief or value is being challenged, because nothing is more likely to trigger defensive reactions. In relationships we *do* get challenged. That's how we get the chance to let go of outmoded behaviour!

If you will only risk lowering your defences, you may find that your partner becomes more accessible and co-operative.

So soften up a little, soldier, and allow yourself to be touched.

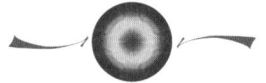

7

CHANGE

Smooth seas do not make skillful sailors.

AFRICAN PROVERB

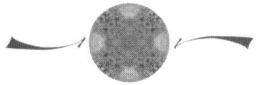

Change is the threshold to the new.

YOU ARE PROBABLY 'ON ALERT'. The familiar is being disturbed as the wind of change blows through your relationship.

It may take the form of a strong wind, testing the strength of the roots of whatever you have planted, or of a hurricane, ripping up everything you've built so far.

If we were totally in tune with our natural rhythms, change would pass us by without distress, in the same way that we accept the passing of the seasons.

But most of us are creatures of habit, preferring to hold on to what we know, even when it is no longer for our own good. We try to stop the wind by blowing back at it. And it is our *resistance* to change, our holding on, that blocks the flow of things and creates an inner stress.

Where this is the case, change may mean discomfort, for it demands that, for a while, we accept the uncertainty, and perhaps chaos, of the unknown.

It is the nature of all living things to be either growing or decaying. There is nothing else. And decay is not bad. It's merely a changing of form. Nothing is lost. The decay of one structure always feeds the development of something new.

The Change card indicates transformation and growth: a time to let go of control and be open to the new, rather than mourning the old. Look for the green shoots of new possibilities. Search in places you have never looked before. The wind of change can uncover what was hidden.

Don't be concerned about what is happening. Rest assured that, as you move into unexplored territory, all is as it should be. There is nothing for you to do but wait and see what will evolve.

Wonder at the transformation of a caterpillar into a butterfly. Before any birth there is a period of waiting.

INVERSE

*We cannot push the river without
going against our nature.*

You seem to have an innate dissatisfaction with the way things are. Perhaps you feel it's your partner, or your relationship, or maybe you are upset by a particular aspect of yourself.

This dissatisfaction is causing you to want to make changes. But the changes you want are more to do with your own agenda than with what needs to happen – and perhaps that's nothing at all!

The task you face in this situation is to allow any change to happen in its own time and in its own way, rather than trying to force it through.

Put your metaphorical feet up and 'let it be'.

8

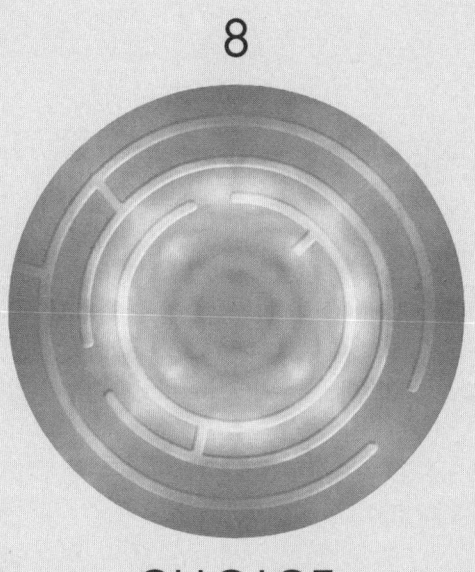

CHOICE

*The only traps are those
we make ourselves.*

Recognizing we have choice is recognizing that our lives are our own.

Do YOU FEEL STUCK or trapped? Have you adopted the belief that this is the way things are and the way they have to be? Or are you sitting on the fence, unconsciously hoping that, by giving yourself time, circumstances will dictate what you should do?

What's being reflected here is precisely your ability and need to choose.

We *always* have choice within a relationship, even if we don't use it. But we are often held back from acting on it by a sense of powerlessness.

Realizing that you have a choice is a matter of maturity. Using that freedom of choice is a matter of empowerment.

What may be holding you back from exercising your ability to choose is fear of making a mistake. Relax! There are no wrong choices: only different ones.

Choose 'A' and you will have certain experiences; choose 'B' and you will have others. Who's to say which are the better? They are simply experiences and whichever you choose, they will help you to grow and learn more about yourself and others.

Don't fall into the trap of believing that you only have a certain number of opportunities in life. It is never the right time to compromise yourself. Your purpose is to fulfil your potential, to grow – not to be limited by negative beliefs about yourself.

Make your choice by considering each option in terms of the question: 'Is this for my highest good?' The situation is challenging you to seize your destiny in both hands and decide on your direction.

Wisdom means seeing each crisis as an opportunity. Don't let *this* opportunity slip through your fingers.

INVERSE

Sometimes the right choice is not to make one.

MAYBE THIS IS NOT THE RIGHT TIME for you to be making choices. There are things hidden which need to come to the surface before you can make a healthy decision. Time will bring more information and better understanding.

We often feel pressurized by ourselves and others to make decisions before we are ready. But time can adjust our perspective, if we will only let it.

Sit back. Relax. Observe what is really going on in yourself and others, without trying to do anything with what you see. Let go of any sense of: 'I have to.' Whose voice is that, anyway?

Tell your partner that you are not ready to make any decisions at the moment. Then watch what happens. Most of all, watch yourself. You might be surprised at the wealth of understanding you can gain by just doing nothing!

9

COMMUNICATION

There are few relationships that would not benefit from a little more communication and a little less guesswork.

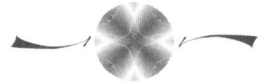

Communication is at the heart of a relationship. For it is in sharing ourselves that we really connect.

YOU APPEAR TO BE WITHHOLDING something from your partner. And in not sharing, you have donned a mask which has created a barrier between you.

This is a time to communicate, communicate again, and then communicate some more. So say whatever you don't want to say. Say why you didn't want to say it. Then say what you *feel* about saying it!

Words are a way to connect and build bridges to the people we love. Real closeness in a relationship is founded on honest communication. We need to know what is going on for one another – it's the only way to prevent misunderstanding and fantasy creeping in.

You need to beware of hiding your thoughts and feelings. It can become a destructive habit, as can expecting a partner to know, telepathically, what is going on. They are both ways of avoiding something –

of trying not to rock the boat while clutching onto an illusion of safety.

But life is *not* safe, and sometimes the boat *has* to be rocked. In speaking your truth you do face risks – primarily that your partner may argue or reject what you are saying. It's best to simply accept that you can't control your partner's response or the situation.

Feel what needs to be said and stay in touch with those feelings while you talk. Let what you say come from your heart, not your head.

Speak the unspeakable. And face the unknowable …

INVERSE

Without silence there can be no listening. Without listening there can be no communication.

COMMUNICATION HAS TWO SIDES to it, and your issue appears to be receptivity.

Perhaps you haven't been allowing someone a chance to get a word in, while you grind on incessantly from your own perspective. Or maybe you just aren't giving others your full attention when they do speak. It could be that you need to learn both when to contain your opinions and how to truly listen when others are talking. You can't know what is going on in other people's minds until they tell you!

Being receptive is about more than just hearing the words. It's about paying attention, listening *without judgement,* and choosing whether to respond or not. You might try *not* responding. It's often not necessary to 'fix' things for other people. Just being there is enough.

Some people can express their deepest feelings in a few moments. Others struggle to know what is going on inside.

Give your partner some space. Encourage him or her to speak. Then shut up, pay attention and, before you say anything, try to get a sense of the real intention behind your words.

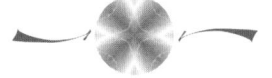

10

EMPATHY

Love is but the discovery of ourselves in others, and the delight in the recognition.

ALEXANDER SMITH

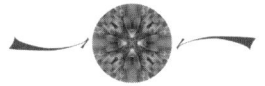

Empathy is the deep understanding we can have for other people. It springs from our ability to recognize ourselves in them – and them in us.

EMPATHY IS THE BRIDGE of the heart that spans the differences between people. It enables a two-way traffic of feelings and experiences, unrestricted by the 'border guards' of judgement and rejection. It links us to our partners through absolute acceptance of each other's realities.

You need to check out if you are being either dismissive or judgemental of your partner's feelings. Maybe you believe that you can avoid unnecessary confrontation by not paying attention to them. Or are you under the impression that if you stop to listen to your partner's point of view, you will need to agree with it?

Empathizing does not necessarily mean agreeing with someone. It's feeling behind the words and understanding what it's like to be in that position.

Are you finding it hard to really acknowledge your partner in this situation? You may have strong beliefs about how people should think or feel. Or perhaps you feel things have to be sorted out one way or the other. Maybe just accepting the differences between you is a new idea.

You might even be concerned that your partner's feelings will overwhelm you if you don't stand back from them. But empathy is not about losing yourself in the depths of someone else's feelings. On the contrary, you very much need to stay in touch with your own. It's essential, though, to sometimes lay aside your personal perspective and beliefs – to let go of your 'position' and just *be there* for someone else. When you do, you may begin to have a rather different picture to the one you are presently seeing.

Sometimes you need to try out empathy very consciously to discover just how potent and useful it is. You not only stand to gain a deeper understanding of your partner's feelings, but also to strengthen the bonds between you.

INVERSE

Sometimes we give what we want to receive.

YOU PROBABLY BELIEVE yourself to be a wonderfully supportive and understanding partner – perhaps even the ideal partner! However, the time has come to question your apparently admirable behaviour.

Empathy is a double-edged sword. For while you may be seen as a great friend and listener, you could be unaware of a deeper, less selfless motive. Isn't your own desire to be needed and loved behind your behaviour? Isn't there a voice inside that sometimes whispers 'What about me?' Moreover, in being so supportive and trying to make yourself indispensable, you may have become a crutch for someone's dependency.

You must learn to be your own therapist first, and stop immersing yourself in other people's problems. Turn your ability to be empathetic, inwards. Only through supporting yourself can you become truly compassionate to others. Stop being so understanding of other people, and understand yourself a little more!

11

EXPRESSION

Show what you are or else deprive the world – and worse, deprive yourself.

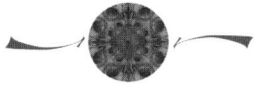

Expression is letting how you feel on the inside show on the outside.

You might want to consider your immediate response to drawing this card – or lack of it! For your challenge is to allow a more demonstrative you to come forward.

You probably believe that you are naturally quite inexpressive or reserved, and may even consider it a quality. But in reality it is one of the ways you have learned to protect yourself, and the situation is asking you to drop this somewhat colourless behaviour so that you can be seen, known and possibly loved a little more.

Being contained, restrained and generally 'cool' may be an image that works in the movies, but it's definitely a problem in real-life relationships. Why should someone who says 'I'm really happy', but whose body language says something else, be believed? How would *you* feel if a person you cared about acted towards you in such an expressionless way?

Withholding expression is not a sign of maturity in a relationship. True maturity is demonstrated by a richness of expression – including the spontaneous expressiveness of the child.

So how about facing the fact that you're scared of showing too much of yourself, in case you get rejected?

The Expression card is not so much about speaking your mind as about allowing your heart to have a face. Through touch, gesture and actions. Through hugging for no reason. Through smiling without words. Through letting the tears come. And singing in the bath occasionally!

You have far greater depth than you have acknowledged – so how about revealing some of it? Take this as an opportunity to show more of the real you, rather than as a threat to the person that you think you should be.

INVERSE

When expression is used to manipulate others, its origin is emotional, not based on true feeling.

DRAMA IS THE WORD that comes to mind – or more accurately, melodrama. You seem to be good at it and, worryingly, a very good actor can get to *believe* in both character and script.

Look deep into your heart. There must be a sense that all is not well. There is an incongruence between how you're behaving and the feelings inside. Your way of expression is being used to control your partner and perhaps mask your true feelings, even from yourself.

It makes no difference whether you are exhibiting joy or sadness, anger or friendship: it is an *act*. Look deeper and you will see that there is a distinct lack of reality in your expression.

How about stepping back and simply containing your emotions for a while? It is only through making contact with your own truth and learning to express it that you will grow: not through manipulating your partner.

12

FREEDOM

Freedom is the uncovering of what has always been there.

STEPHEN LEVINE

To be free is to realize that nothing external is controlling us.

Too often we suffer from the illusion that we have no free will. In reality we are all free. Yet we do not believe it – or do not want to. As a result we can feel imprisoned within a relationship and see our partner as the jailer.

In choosing this card, you are asked to reflect on a deeply held belief that you are not in control of your own destiny.

Take an honest look at your life and your relationships and ask yourself in what ways you believe you are not free. See how you were free to make the choices you made, and are free to make different ones now.

What you may not have recognized is that all choices have consequences. And perhaps it is these that feel like they are trapping you.

Recognizing your freedom will not free you from

consequences, but it *will* free you from feeling powerless, enabling you to take mature responsibility.

There is such safety in the familiar comfort and security of our 'prison' that we argue fiercely to defend our need to stay there. Like a bird that's been caged too long, when the cage door is opened we may prefer to stay inside, squawking our displeasure, rather than accept that we are choosing to stay there.

The only real cost of freedom is letting go of the benefits of imprisonment!

As long as you remain blind to the fact that you are your own inner jailer and any restrictions in your life are self-imposed, you'll continue to feel others are dictating the course of your life. And in relationships you will either keep blaming your partner for your imprisonment, or be waiting for another partner to 'free' you.

Take heart. As soon as you really believe that you hold the key, a feeling of freedom will begin to permeate every aspect of your life.

INVERSE

*To discover that commitment is not a jailer
is to know freedom in a relationship.*

MAYBE YOU BELIEVE that relationships chain you and that you can only be free on your own. Do you fear that the ongoing presence of another person in your life would diminish your choices and hold you back?

The truth is that no-one can ever bind you – even in the most committed of relationships you will always be free.

Look back over your relationships and you may find a theme of 'loving and leaving'. How real were your reasons for leaving? Did you really try to work things out, or were you just escaping from yourself, running from the things you needed to face?

The challenge may be for you to *stay* with the situation you are in, even though every cell in your body is screaming at you to quit. What you may perceive as restlessness or a need not to be tied down is based on avoidance. Could it be that you are scared of intimacy, frightened of staying around long enough to risk loving and being loved? It may be that leaving simply postpones the day when you have to grow up and finally face your fears.

Put the brakes on. Have you truly done all you can to make this relationship work? See if you can bring your free spirit and love of variety *into* your relationship rather than letting them lead you out.

13

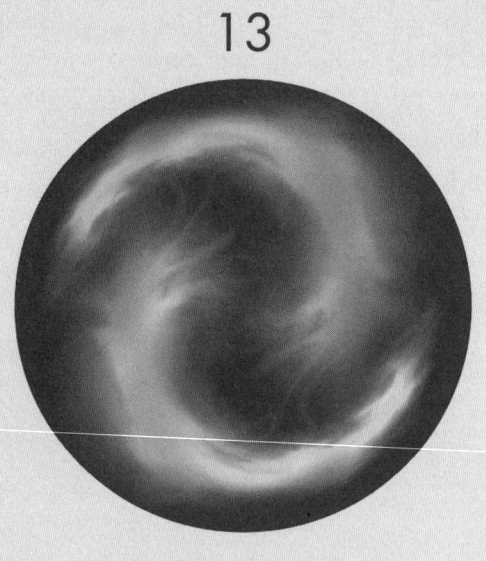

FRIENDSHIP

Love is blind, but friendship closes its eyes.

Real friendship provides the space for two people to meet as equals, with mutual respect, honesty and care.

BEING IN A RELATIONSHIP requires the adaptability to move between different roles. Once these roles are understood, a fluid way of relating can evolve. The most crucial of all the roles is friendship – but sadly its importance can easily be overlooked.

Friendship is the bottom line, the cornerstone of all good relationships. Without it there is no resting place, no solid foundation on which to build and no point at which to meet as equals.

Consider whether you have established a relationship that excludes simple friendship. And question what role you are playing: lover, parent, child, sibling? How would you be dealing differently with the situation if this were a close friendship rather than your intimate relationship?

All relationships are deepened by risk and it seems you need to risk moving into a position of equality with your partner. You might fear that doing this will threaten some other aspect of the relationship – perhaps romance or the balance of power. Or you could be concerned that by being friends you will lose the element of spice. But friendship threatens nothing – except illusion.

Drop whatever role you are caught in. Try being your partner's friend for a while and see how equality can change the dynamic.

INVERSE

True friendship stands up to examination – and benefits from it.

YOUR RELATIONSHIP APPEARS TO be suffering from the effects of 'collusion' – an unspoken agreement between you. You need to examine the set of beliefs that you and your partner silently share and think about whether you have constructed a 'safe space' to protect the relationship, that precludes the depths and heights of a full-blooded partnership.

This 'safe space' probably evolved from a shared experience of genuine closeness, which you then suspended in time, in an attempt to permanently glue the relationship together. There is a sense here of two scared children holding hands in a dark wood, acting brave in order to reassure each other.

Rather than dealing directly with the real issue in the relationship, you are probably walking around it, in order to protect the 'close friendship' you share, and are then wondering why nothing is getting resolved.

This 'us against the world' form of relationship can eradicate other more mature aspects of a partnership and make true intimacy impossible, even though it *feels* intimate, or at least cosy! For in the long run such cosiness becomes stifling, destroying many opportunities for growth.

Tackling this issue is a challenge because you will feel the foundations of the relationship being threatened. And there's a tendency for the person who takes the first tenuous step out of such collusion to be seen by the other as a traitor. You will need both courage and objectivity.

The way forward is to wake up to what you've helped to create and examine your part in it. What are the unspoken words? What is the silent agreement between you? If you don't express your true feelings and desires now, when will you? No matter how painful this may be, something new and eventually more fulfilling *will* result if you can only be honest.

14

HONESTY

*Many admit the truth to themselves,
but few confess it to others.*

INAYAT KHAN

*Honesty is having the courage
to express what we feel, irrespective of the
consequences to ourselves.*

WHAT ARE YOU KEEPING to yourself, not daring to tell? What are you hiding away in some dark corner, hoping it won't be discovered?

You seem to be more concerned about what might happen if you were honest, than with the truth itself.

A lack of honesty usually indicates there is a fear of the consequences. Perhaps you are concerned you will get hurt if you tell the truth. Or maybe you're afraid that if you share what's on your mind, you'll alienate or hurt someone. Either way, you can be sure it's primarily yourself you are protecting.

Whenever there is lying or the withholding of feelings in a relationship, a separation is created. Partners register it deep inside and feel uncomfortable. And over time, the distancing creates a barrier to intimacy.

Honesty is essential for a happy relationship. The more open you can be, the closer you will feel. It means you can both relax, knowing all there is to know, and *be real*.

Clarify what it is you need to admit or reveal. Then decide how you're going to deal with it. Honesty makes different demands in different situations.

It could be that you need to arm yourself with the fiery sword of truth, to cut through a confused tangle of emotions or unspoken feelings. If you are unused to being a 'warrior of truth', you may need courage to stand your ground and not be deflected from what you need to express.

Or it may be that this card is challenging you to drop your defences and say what is going on for you, knowing that the consequences may be painful.

Whatever the demand, let go of all expectations of the outcome. Control and honesty do not go hand in hand.

No matter what happens, no matter what anyone else thinks or does, you will know that you have dared to be real and done the very best you could.

INVERSE

The sword of truth is a powerful weapon that can cut deeply. It should only be used when the hand that wields it is connected to the heart.

PERHAPS YOU NEVER THOUGHT that you could be too honest, but you are certainly being asked to consider that now.

There are times when it is not appropriate to say all you know or feel about something, and it seems this is one of them. Maybe you have been using honesty in a distorted or insensitive way, to belittle or criticize, or to gossip about other people?

If you are not sure whether you have been abusing others in the name of honesty, think about your intention. Has your truthfulness been helpful, or damaging? Have you used it lovingly to give or gain clarity, or maliciously to hurt, to gain power or feel self-righteous?

Could it be your *own* feelings of inadequacy that are causing you to cut others down to size? Perhaps the honesty that's needed is to yourself, about yourself.

15

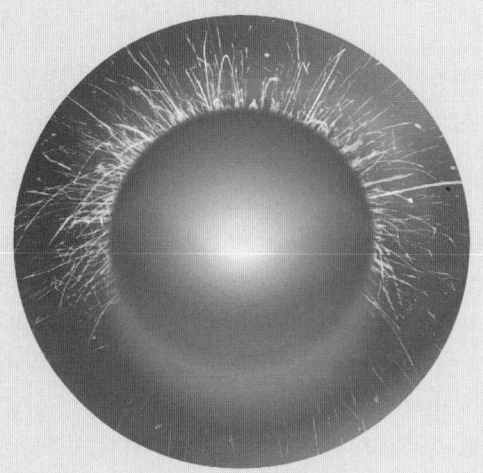

HUMOUR

Life is like a mirror.
We get the best results
when we smile at it.

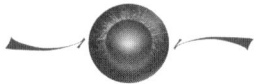

Humour releases us from the isolation of self-protection, providing an opportunity for our hearts to open again.

YOU MAY BE FEELING that your situation is no laughing matter, but consider whether you are too concerned with protecting yourself. There is a strong connection between defensiveness and an absence of humour, and it seems that in shielding your heart you have also darkened it, losing your ability to be light-hearted.

Do you remember the light-heartedness that you and your partner shared when you were first together? That capacity is still there. Take a step back and look for the humour in your present predicament. It's only when you drop your defences that you can discover the funny side and touch each other through humour.

Think about a time when you collapsed with laughter. You will be remembering your defences collapsing, for humour has the wonderful ability to open up the heart, sweeping away self-protection and self-consciousness.

Humour draws us away from fears of what might happen. It takes us off the pedestal of defensive self-righteousness and makes us see ourselves for the confused, all-too-human individuals we really are. The purest humour invariably arises when we stop taking ourselves so seriously and acknowledge our fault-riddled natures.

Try to introduce a fresh perspective to your situation. Even the most serious problems don't necessarily have to be dealt with in a serious way. Allowing humour in doesn't mean you aren't hurting – laughter and tears are familiar companions. But it can break the tension and provide a welcome relief from anxiety.

If you think that humour might compromise your position; that you might lose face or power, then maybe that is exactly what you need to experience, to discover just how worthless they are.

Historically, a comedy was a play where the hero or heroine triumphed over adversity. Perhaps you haven't considered that letting go and seeing the comedy of your situation could signal a similar victory.

Perhaps it's time you tried …

INVERSE

When humour is used to mask deeper feelings, laughter has a hollow ring.

You are being asked whether you are making light of something that, for your own sake, demands a more serious attitude. Perhaps you feel that people shouldn't make mountains out of molehills; that life's too short for such intensity and that this problem can be laughed off.

Humour can be used as a way to avoid dealing with something. Many great comedians are depressives who developed their art to help them block out the inner pain. But ultimately, we have to face the pain.

Who or what are you brushing off so lightly? What is it that's so difficult for you to face?

Underneath your attempt at light-heartedness are feelings that you seem intent on avoiding, and are trying to tuck away into a dark corner. The trouble is, such feelings will not go away. They'll remain as a weight on your heart until you have the courage to deal with them. And a heavy heart leaves little space for anything but shallow laughter.

If making fun of things is a habit, getting in touch with your deeper feelings may take effort on your part, for you will have a belief that those feelings are in some way wrong. But your situation is demanding that you acknowledge the mask you are wearing and choose instead to reveal your true face.

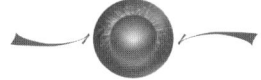

16

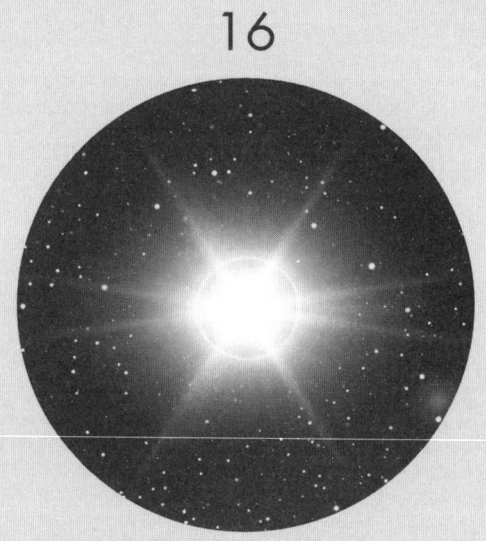

INDEPENDENCE

*Most seek to be lost in the 'two in one',
but it is the finding of the One in two
that is the prize.*

Independence comes from knowing we can depend on ourselves. It gives us the strength to stand apart, trusting in the power of our individuality.

THE SITUATION YOU ARE IN seems to have arisen from your dependency on your partner. You are probably feeling neglected and wanting more of your partner's attention or time. Perhaps you feel threatened because your partner is pulling away from your clinginess.

Think about how children who are insecure constantly seek attention and affirmation by tugging at their mothers' clothes. Ask yourself how you, too, may be demonstrating such behaviour in your own way.

Dependency can be a web that we weave to hold on to another person. But ultimately we become entangled in it ourselves, not knowing how else to relate.

Of course you want to feel supported in your relationship, but when your need for support goes beyond what is offered, it turns instead to neediness.

To gain a real and lasting sense of independence, you need to find your own mature qualities of strength and self-reliance. This is a major step on the path of self-love and a huge stride towards being able to truly love another person, without clinging or constantly needing help or attention. Only when you have taken this step will you be able to move freely between the poles of separateness and togetherness with a partner.

Consider the eagle as a powerful metaphor for independence in a relationship. A mated pair fly with great distance between them, yet always within view of each other. Each is in their own power, not shadowed by the other. Together, but separate.

INVERSE

Refusing to ask for or accept help is a sign of pride, not independence.

THE INDEPENDENT STANCE you are taking at the moment stems from your unwillingness to ask for support, rather than from real strength of character.

Do you ever ask for help? Do you even recognize that you need some support now? Self-sufficiency can go to extremes and become a habit hard to break. Perhaps you expect others to telepathically know when you need their help? Or are you using your 'independence' to martyr yourself and so manipulate your partner through guilt?

Wanting to go it alone, to be a hero or to prove yourself, mask both a need to be in control and a fear of trusting someone. So you will be showing true courage if you can ask for some support now.

There are times when partners need to lean on each other and accept loving help. It's one of the gifts of relationships and an opportunity for greater closeness.

17

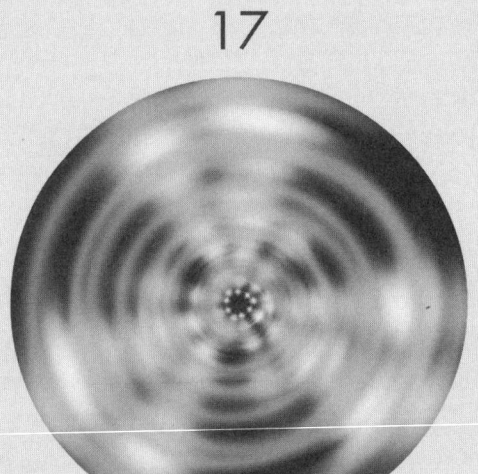

INITIATING

*Whatever you can do,
or dream you can, begin it.
Boldness has genius, power
and magic in it; begin it now.*

JOHANN WOLFGANG VON GOETHE

Initiating takes us from the safety of passivity to creativity. It is this daring to move away from security that is the 'initiation' – the crossing of a threshold into full participation in life.

IT SEEMS YOU ARE not taking the lead when it is clearly time for you to do so. Maybe it scares you to make the first move, and risk getting things wrong. Or perhaps you've just become lazy!

But aren't you fed up with being a follower? Repeatedly letting other people take responsibility weakens your presence in the world. And in a relationship you end up playing the helpless child or condemning what your partner does from a place of safety on the sidelines.

Are you too attached to being seen as nice or easy-going, to dare to stand up and stand out? Or could it be that you equate taking the initiative with being bossy or aggressive? We find the best of reasons to hide!

In the past you may have been discouraged when you tried to make decisions and take the lead. Perhaps you were belittled for getting it wrong when you seized the initiative. Or maybe you were told not to be so pushy, and encouraged to stay in the background.

Whatever it was, it's time to update your beliefs and reclaim your spirit of adventure. Everyone gets it wrong sometimes, but that's no reason to relinquish control of your life!

Think of the situation you're facing as a potential painting. You can either do 'painting by numbers', where someone else defines the content and the shapes, and you may (if you're lucky) get to do some colouring in. Or you can choose to paint your own picture which, irrespective of artistic merit, will be yours and yours alone.

As with any creative act, you have to be prepared to take risks. So make that initial mark and don't be surprised if you end up with a result you didn't expect.

To keep on growing you need to dare to break habits. Stop being a passenger in your own life and get into the driver's seat!

INVERSE

Letting someone else take the reins is a lesson in trust.

You seem to be using your natural qualities of leadership in a way that blocks or overrides your partner's feelings.

When you have a talent for something, it's tempting to use it, regardless. The challenge is to learn when and how to use it.

Consider whether you are being a bit bossy at the moment, expecting others to play your games, and sulking or getting angry if they won't. And ask yourself why you find it so difficult to let someone else take the initiative from time to time.

Is it hard for you to put yourself in someone else's hands? Are you concerned that you will miss out on something if you step back – or be bored? Or do you just hate the thought of not having control?

Take an honest look at yourself and think about whether your need to initiate is rooted in your heart or your need for power. Put yourself in your partner's position and ponder on the suppressive effect your behaviour is probably having.

It's time to try listening to others and exchanging ideas. Remember that each of us is unique. By encouraging and being open to your partner's input, you will find your horizons broadening, and you may discover new ways of enjoying yourself!

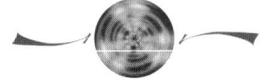

18

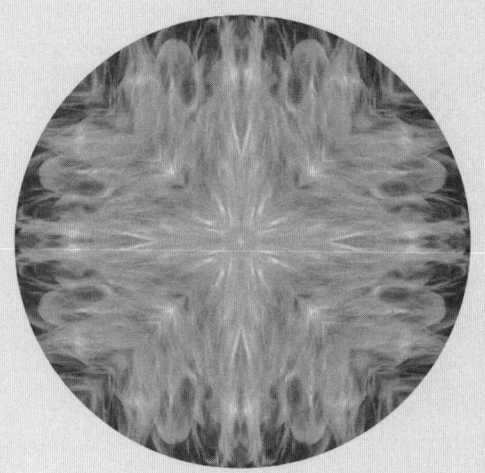

INTEGRITY

*Men stumble over the truth from
time to time,
but most pick themselves up
and hurry off as if nothing has happened.*

WINSTON CHURCHILL

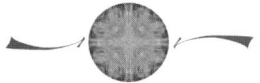

Integrity calls for respect, not only for ourselves, but for everyone else as part of the whole. It springs from the pure essence of honesty, from a heart that is undivided and cannot be swayed by others or by the desire for gain.

To act with integrity, you need to listen to the still, small voice deep within that tells you what is right. For integrity cannot be found outside yourself.

It is often in childhood that we are driven to compromise our authentic expression. Prompted by the need for approval, we lose touch with our personal integrity. The voice within that knows the truth becomes muffled, even silenced. And our innate integrity is replaced by a learned morality and code of behaviour.

As an adult you are faced now with the challenge of once more embodying your integrity, this time with full consciousness of what you are doing. Your inner voice is speaking, but you may need to quieten yourself in order to hear it.

What is happening in your life that is demanding your integrity? Is there something going on that you would rather not share – something you don't feel happy about deep down? If so, are you prepared to take responsibility, or are you kidding yourself that you have no choice?

You may be feeling tempted to read a letter that's private, to share a confidence, break a promise or withhold something in order to save face. Perhaps you're feeling guilty for already having done so.

If you've been keeping something a secret, you might need to reveal it, to clear the way forward. Or this time you may just have to suffer in silence, using the experience as a lesson learned for the future.

Integrity means saying 'No' to what feels dishonest or unkind or merely expedient, and calls for strength in the face of temptation. It can also mean saying 'Yes' to what may feel difficult or challenging.

It is usually emotions that lure us away from the path of integrity. So, if there's a churning or tightness in your stomach, then it's likely that fear, anger, jealousy or desire is trying to lead you astray.

If you are unsure what action to take, try to base your choice not on emotional desire or short-term gain but on what feels right inside. What's right may seem more painful or scary in the immediate future, but take heart and know that ultimately it will be what serves you best on your life's path.

INVERSE

Self-righteousness demands a review of our beliefs, and the courage to be open-minded.

SMUG AND MORALIZING. Is it possible this could be you? For these are the symptoms of a lost inner voice, one that lies buried beneath judgements and opinions inherited from others.

You seem to be creating a feeling of safety by perching loftily on a mountain of rigidly held views. But where did they come from? And how are you so sure of yourself?

We often feel safer when we moralize to others from inherited or conventional beliefs, rather than risking discovering our own – and perhaps finding we have nothing to say.

The Integrity card inverted asks you to stop being so opinionated, and be open to revising what you presently think to be true.

Ease up and soften into the place of 'not knowing' for a while. Even now, that still, small voice is speaking to you, if you will only listen.

19

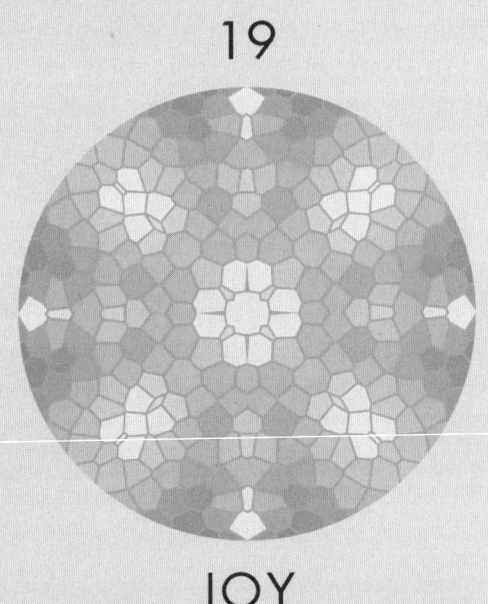

JOY

It is far more nourishing to eat the feast of life than simply to read the menu.

MICK CSAKY

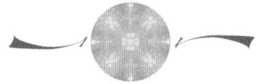

Joy is only possible when we surrender to the richness of the moment.

THE EXTRAORDINARY THING about joy is how little we allow it. Yet is it surprising when, as happy, excited children, we were so often told to 'be quiet' or 'behave'? No wonder we fear it will be snatched away if we let it through!

So many of us suffer from the belief that we need to feel safe before we can allow ourselves to be joyful. And since relationships often *don't* feel safe, joy can become a distant prize to attain 'one day'.

Maybe you're questioning where the joy is in your relationship, but the chances are that this situation will be familiar to you, even from when you were single. For joy is not 'out there'. It's in you, and it always has been. You have just shrouded it with fears and negative beliefs.

Joy is the most ephemeral of feelings and only exists in the moment.

Are you focusing on problems and overlooking the possibilities for pleasure that surround you in the here and now?

Choose to let go of trying to figure everything out. You've never succeeded before, and nothing is about to change in that direction! Then, focus on something that brings you pure, simple, mindless pleasure. It may be connected to your relationship, or something you do on your own.

Whatever it is, engage with it completely, to the exclusion of everything else. Live your enjoyment, whether it be by releasing your body in dance, gazing at something of beauty, or walking at dawn.

Young children abound with joy, simply because they don't feel the need to worry about the future and sort things out. This brings them solidly into the present, where they can fully experience the living moment. They jump *for* joy and *with* joy: to reach it and because of it.

Underneath your shroud, the joyful child is still alive within you, waiting and wanting to be freed. It cannot be freed by anyone other than yourself.

Don't waste your energy regretting the past or fearing the future. Rejoice in the now and free that child!

INVERSE

There is a great difference between feeling joy and acting happy. Where joy can quietly suffuse our beings, without anyone else knowing we're feeling it, acting happy is an ongoing performance to convince ourselves and manipulate others.

THOUGH YOU CAN NEVER have too much joy in your life, if you choose to have only that feeling, then the chances are you are avoiding something.

Are you playing the 'joyful being' to avoid uncomfortable feelings? If so, you will doubtless be perceiving some of the people in your life as the opposite – as dark and brooding, argumentative or pessimistic. The more you exaggerate your 'lightness', the more you will get locked into polarizing others as 'dark' and fail to understand either yourself or them.

Initially this may be hard for you to grasp. For surely

joy is one of the great treasures of life, and why on earth would you not want to express it? But not expressing it isn't the issue. The issue is to allow space for other feelings, too.

It is only through recognizing and allowing the full breadth of your own feelings that you will be able to relate fully to another individual – and discover a depth of joy you may never have known.

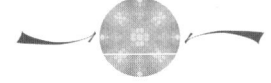

20

LETTING GO

If you love something, let it go.
If it comes back, it's yours.
If it doesn't, it never was.

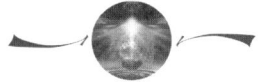

*Letting go is releasing that which
no longer benefits us.*

THIS CARD INDICATES that you need to consciously let go of something, someone, a way of being, or even all three! Whatever it is, you have outgrown the need for it, but are finding it difficult to release.

Besides clinging out of habit, what ties us to things and people we have outgrown is primarily the fear that if we let go, nothing and no-one will ever take their place. So we dig in our heels and hold tight to what we know.

When one door closes, another door opens, and this card is symbolic of a progressive change that is waiting to happen. But only you can initiate it by releasing the old, and thereby making space for the new.

This is probably a stressful and confusing time for you. You may be aware of an inner voice urging you to make the decision to let go, but you are hesitating, sensing you would be moving into unknown territory. Perhaps you're struggling to hold on to something or somebody. Maybe you're fighting off the inevitable. Either way, you must be feeling tired from all the effort!

In situations like this, it is tempting to hope that time, a magical being or the universe will intercede, removing the need for us to act. But that is precisely what cannot happen, when the need is to learn about letting go and plunging into the unknown. If we always played safe, we would end up going round a very small circle of experiences, learning very little.

It seems like you are sitting on a raft on a fast-flowing river, but you are still by the bank and holding on to a branch. Perhaps you can see a few boulders downstream that look hazardous. You are understandably concerned at leaving this place of safety; worried where the river will take you and whether you can survive the rocky ride. But the river knows where it's going, for this is your river of life.

Allow it to take you where you need to be. And allow, too, the feelings that are a part of any letting go.

Let go, and trust …

INVERSE

Giving in is the collapse of the self under the pressure of another.

What do you want to happen here? Are you letting something slip through your fingers without a protest? Are you really going with the flow or just meekly following the path of least resistance and letting someone else call all the shots? Could it be that your low self-esteem is undermining your authority?

You may feel like you're being very understanding and easy-going. But with your hands up in a gesture of surrender, you could easily be robbed of what is rightfully yours, or taken somewhere you don't want to go.

Stop saying 'It doesn't matter' or 'I don't mind' when, deep down, it does, and you do.

Sometimes we are faced with situations where we have to fight to keep what we have or for what we want. Not with anger, desperation or wild emotion, but through clearly expressed feelings and strong boundaries.

Review what is happening. Don't let anything happen that you don't want to happen, without protest. You may not get what you want, but that isn't the point. The point is that you engage with the situation rather than stand back in mute acceptance.

21

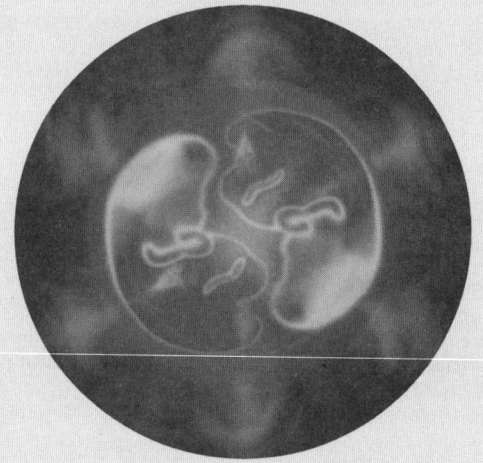

NURTURE

*As we affirm who we are,
we become who we are.*

ANNE WILSON SCHAEF

*Nurture is whatever we take in that strengthens
us and helps us to grow.
How well we nurture ourselves reflects how good
we feel about ourselves.*

We all need to feel cared for. But our primary source of care has to be ourselves. This is a core lesson and one that must be faced in order for us to relate healthily to others and ourselves, from a base of strength.

If we are unable to really nurture ourselves, there's a danger we will become dependent on our partners, expecting them to 'feed' us and, quite possibly, draining them in the process. Or we will choose partners who are incapable of loving, confirming our belief that it is not possible for us to be loved.

The situation that you are in is calling for you to differentiate between what nurtures you and what doesn't. The familiar and the emotionally desirable are not necessarily of benefit to you, even though they may be holding the strongest attraction.

You are being asked first to recognize, then to act on your need for proper nurturing.

The only way to do this is by caring for yourself as if you were the most precious person on earth.

Get in touch with your deepest needs and seek, as best you can, to supply them for yourself. Once you can do that, it will become more apparent how to really sustain others, without a hidden agenda.

If you can only receive the support that these words offer, it will be nurturing in itself. Should you feel a resistance, notice that you find it hard to believe that you should care for yourself, and perhaps acknowledge: 'If I don't think I'm worth nurturing, why should anyone else?'

Paradoxically, you will only begin to attract a caring response from your partner when you demonstrate a genuine capacity to care for yourself.

INVERSE

Self-indulgence is pandering to our own fancies and desires, to the exclusion of others.

WHAT DO YOU BELIEVE would happen if you redirected to your partner some of the attention that you're lavishing on yourself? There is a great difference between really caring for yourself and being selfish.

You need to find a way to feed your hungry heart from within, so that you will have more of yourself to give and share. At present it seems that every time you give your partner something instead of giving it to yourself, you feel like you're suffering a loss. But you will find that once it is given from the heart, without expectation, you will receive something greater back.

Are you starving your partner – of love, of care, of you? How different things would be if only you could let go of the idea that you are losing out, and do something that your partner would really appreciate and benefit from. However, if you are going to do it, make sure it's from your heart.

22

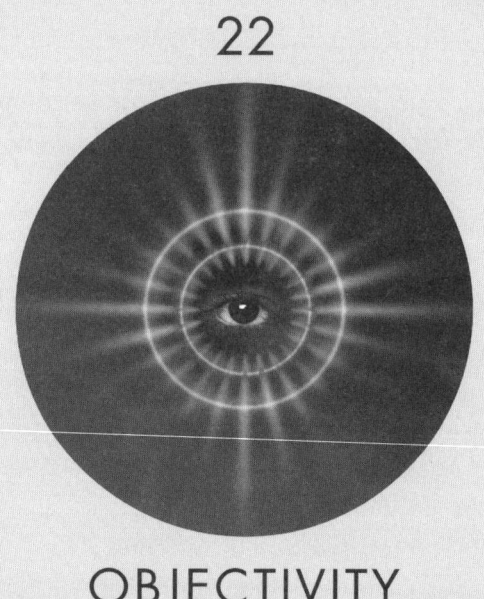

OBJECTIVITY

*If you're drowning, it's worth spending
a moment checking which way is up.*

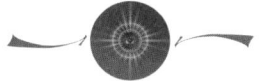

Objectivity is the ability to step back from our emotions in order to gain a clearer perspective. By moving away from subjectivity, we can see our own and others' behaviour free of emotional distortion.

YOU APPEAR TO BE so involved in the emotional drama of your situation that you have lost sight of the broader picture.

Are you feeling stuck or confused and finding yourself reacting to other people, rather than choosing your own direction?

What's needed is an overview of what is happening. If you only identify with your emotions, you lose perspective on your life. And you may well be overwhelmed by your own or your partner's emotional reactions.

Clarity comes from being in the place of the wise, objective observer, that part of us that cannot be pulled or pushed but merely sees.

Imagine yourself stepping out of the drama of your

life for a while. Come down off the stage and spend some time sitting in the audience, watching yourself and the other actors in the play. For wisdom lies in objectivity.

What is the plot here? What are the intentions of the various characters? How do you feel about them and their behaviour? From this place of wisdom, would you like to change what your character says or does?

Objectivity provides the space to see more clearly through our emotions, not only to the manipulations that may be happening, but also to the beautiful things that we might otherwise miss. It demands maturity, for being subject to our emotions is the place of either the child, who lays the blame on others, or the adolescent, who can't resist the thrill of the emotional roller-coaster.

While a subjective perspective might be: 'He doesn't love me', an objective perspective could be: 'He's scared of loving', or 'I'm very needy of him'. 'I feel worthless' might become: 'I'm scared of succeeding'. How different they sound.

Without objectivity it's easy to feel like a victim, subject to experiences that seem beyond your control.

But once you discover how to step back, you can start to recognize the unhealthy patterns you weave into relationships and learn how they ultimately undermine you.

Become the eagle circling high above the ground, whose vision stretches to the far horizons, yet takes in the smallest detail below. Observe your present situation within the context of the panorama of your life. And recognize that you are the only one with the potential to see your life as it really is.

INVERSE

Aloofness takes us out of life into a realm where we are cut off from our hearts, for fear of feeling too much.

YOU MAY MAKE A wonderful strategist in your ability to see what is happening and plan accordingly, but in that remote place you fail to appreciate the importance of the feelings involved – your own and other people's.

You can pretend feelings don't exist, walk around them, even trample on them. But they are still there: an essential part of who you are. And what they tell you can often be very different to what you *think* about a situation.

It seems you are trying to stay removed from this situation because you believe it to be too painful or challenging to allow your feelings in. Perhaps you consider your feelings to be childish or uncool. You will certainly have created strong reasons not to feel them.

Choosing this card inverted is asking you to let those feelings come forward and be as important in your relationship as your ability to rationalize.

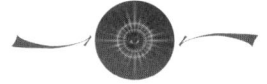

23

REALITY

Truth waits for eyes unclouded by longing.

Seeing through illusion is one of the greatest challenges life presents – and one that few have the courage to take up. Reality is simply what is: the emperor with no clothes; the naked truth.

YOU ARE BEING ASKED to look again at your situation, without viewing it through the distorting filter of your emotional projections or romantic imagination.

When you move away from reality, you move into a world of illusion where hope and fantasy reign. In waiting for everything to turn out alright, real life is put on hold and your desires and expectations blind you to what is actually happening.

Are you deluding yourself; trying to avoid the truth about the situation you're in or your responsibility for it? Are you escaping into fantasies of how your life or your partner could be, if only? Maybe you are being persuaded by someone else's view of reality, or perhaps you've been hooked in by one of the romantic myths.

You may have created a world of make-believe, in order to feel safe and secure in your specialness, and be waiting for someone else to spot this special you. But perhaps it's you who needs to recognize who you are and what you already have. If you're finding it hard to accept the reality of yourself, you may also find it hard to accept any partner, just as they are.

Living in reality means seeing things exactly as they are, free from the desire for them to be different; perceiving the real possibilities or shortcomings of the here and now, instead of fantasizing over some mirage on a distant horizon. It entails having both feet firmly on the ground, rather than living with your head in the clouds.

Picture yourself peering longingly over the fence at someone else's beautiful, landscaped garden, while your own plot is completely overgrown. You may believe life made a mistake in giving you this garden, and may be waiting for it to straighten out on its own. But there are no mistakes. Wake up! Take a look around! Your garden is what you make of it, and you can either find the flowers among the weeds or make the decision to change it. Either way, you need to get your hands dirty and work with the earthy solidity of reality.

While you live in hopes, airily dreaming of what could be, life is passing you by. And relationships will be suffering from your lack of presence. So get back into that body and live the life you have. It may feel like a step down, or a step back, but in reality, it's a step into life.

INVERSE

When realism becomes rigidity, we can be blind to new possibilities.

REALITY IS FOREVER CHANGING. But in your need to feel secure you may have taken what you believe to be the realities of life and frozen them in time, and now you are vigorously defending them.

Are you feeling uneasy with someone else's spontaneity, concerned that things may move out of control? Is it possible that, in sticking rigidly to what you see as the facts of the matter, you have set your beliefs in concrete?

It's true that you're being very down to earth in your thinking. But by blocking your imaginative side, you are severely limiting your possibilities in life. Being realistic doesn't mean saying 'No' to creativity and play. And perhaps you need both in this situation.

Maybe you are scared that you will only be disappointed if you have hopes and dreams, so feel it's safer not to bother. But doesn't that sound sad? As long as you are prepared to work towards expanding your vision, it can become part of your reality, and you may make new discoveries on the way.

But first, you need to dream a little …

24

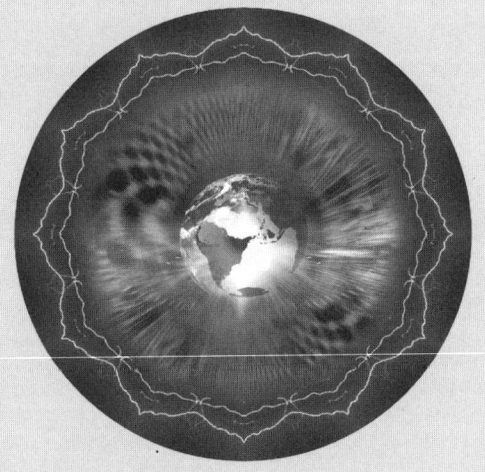

RESPONSIBILITY

*Take your life in your own hands
and what happens?
A terrible thing – no-one to blame.*

ERICA JONG

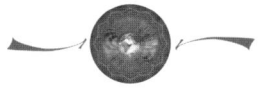

Taking responsibility is the mature acceptance that the only person who controls your life is you.

YOU'RE PROBABLY FEELING HURT or angry at the cards that life has dealt you, or perhaps you don't understand why someone is treating you in a particular way.

There's a tough truth to be learned here that, once understood and consistently applied in all situations, will permanently change your perspective on the world and lead to far more rewarding relationships.

You alone are responsible for *everything* that's happening to you. There's nobody else to blame.

It is only as children that we are entitled to disclaim responsibility. As adults we must assume responsibility, or forever remain children.

Right now, it's time to stop playing the victim, and grow up. The measure of your maturity is how much responsibility you are prepared to take for this situation. Yet it seems you are still wanting others to take care of you and your feelings, or wanting to blame them for your difficulties.

Responsibility is the 'ability to respond', and that can only come if you take back the power you've invested in someone else by being a victim and saying you're not to blame. What if you *were* to blame? Wouldn't that give you greater authority?

Whatever feelings you are having, they are *your* responsibility. No-one can make you feel, do or be anything unless you, at some level, choose to do so. So step back from the issue and ask yourself: 'What part am I playing in this situation?'

If you are wanting to reject this guidance and are thinking you must have drawn the wrong card, you can be sure that it's relevant to you. For a person who takes responsibility would now be searching inside to see how these words are appropriate!

The only payoff for not taking responsibility in this situation is the ability to blame. But is that such a prize to hold on to?

Recognize that you *do* have power and you're big enough to take back the blame!

INVERSE

Guilt is an emotion that we have developed to control one another, and all it does is increase the negativity in the world.

YOU'RE PROBABLY FEELING GUILTY or overly responsible for someone else's feelings. Even if you *have* done or said something that was hurtful, you need to separate the things for which you are responsible from those for which you are not.

This may be hard for you for two reasons. The first is your belief that 'good' people have a sense of conscience. The second is that by thinking you're responsible for others and how they feel, you can avoid taking responsibility for yourself. In other words, you don't have to look inside and be courageous enough to follow your own heart.

What you may need to realize is that guilt is a distortion of responsibility. Not only does it hang the head and sap the spirit, it seeps through the bones, taking away any possibility of joy.

Thinking it's all your fault is of absolutely no benefit to you or anyone else. Instead of shrouding yourself in guilt and blaming yourself for all you've done, learn to take *healthy* responsibility.

First, accept your part in the situation and connect with the feelings of hurt you may have triggered in yourself and others.

Next, express your regret unconditionally.

Finally, let it go – even if someone else doesn't want you to! Punishing yourself is every bit as reprehensible as punishing someone else.

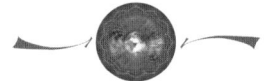

25

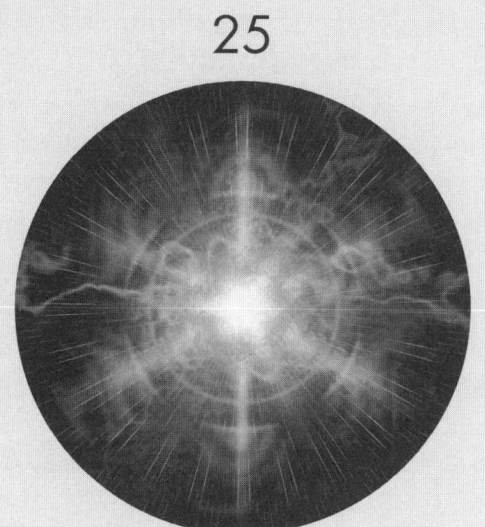

SADNESS

The deeper that sorrow carves into your being, the more joy you can contain.

KAHLIL GIBRAN

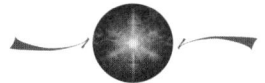

Sadness links us to the deep pain that is a part of being human. By allowing our sadness, we allow the richness of the heart to be expressed.

THERE IS A NATURAL, uncontrollable ebb and flow in all living things; a movement from one opposite to another. Without opposites, there is no movement. Without movement, there is stagnation.

So it is that without the contrast of sadness, joy cannot exist. The two are inextricably linked. When we experience either one of them, our whole being softens and expands. And both lead to the opening of our hearts.

You are being encouraged to feel, really feel, the depths of your sadness. Perhaps you've been putting up a resistance to these feelings, thinking they are a sign of weakness or failure, or maybe you're concerned that once you immerse yourself in them, you will never resurface.

Don't be afraid, or seek to escape from the feelings.

Strange as it may seem, if you can only stay with it, sadness can be a gift and a precious opportunity for healing.

To get more fully in touch with your feelings, give yourself plenty of time and space, preferably on your own. You may first need to soften your attitude towards yourself and accept the situation you're in. The only word of warning is, as much as you can, don't dwell on thoughts about *why* you are sad; just be with the feelings. You may be touching sadness that has been waiting for years to be recognized, and thinking too much can limit the flow of healing.

If you feel like your heart is breaking, it may be partly true. But it is breaking *open*, not breaking into pieces. It is the hard shell that protects your heart that is cracking. And some hearts need many knocks before the shell finally drops away.

In the depths of your pain, you may even feel like you're dying – and in a way you are. But something always has to die in order to make room for new things to come forward …

There is nothing as sad as people who cannot feel their sadness.

INVERSE

Melancholia can become an all-too-familiar friend, with nothing to offer but familiarity.

IT SEEMS THAT YOUR SADNESS has turned to melancholy, and you're wallowing in it rather than allowing it to change.

Where sadness can deepen your connection to the world, in melancholy you turn away from it. Holding on to suffering will eventually alienate others, rather than touch them, and provide you with more reasons to feel down.

When you're not feeling gloomy, you're probably feeling victimized and resentful towards others for 'doing this to you'. But no-one has *done* anything to you. It's how you have chosen to react that is keeping you in this depressed state. In holding on to some painful event that has passed, you may feel unable to move forward. And you may have an unreasonable hope that your melancholy will change things for you. It won't. You'll just get older!

Picture yourself in ten years time, feeling this way. And then in another ten. Is that really what you want?

It's imperative that you set a clear intention around what you truly want now. And then go for it.

Think of a ritual that might help you. Perhaps you could light a candle to symbolize your unhappiness – and let it burn away. Then choose a special candle to symbolize the return of hope, and light it to affirm what you want to bring into your life.

Turn to face the world again, and be open to receive what it can give. Everything is possible, even beyond your wildest dreams.

26

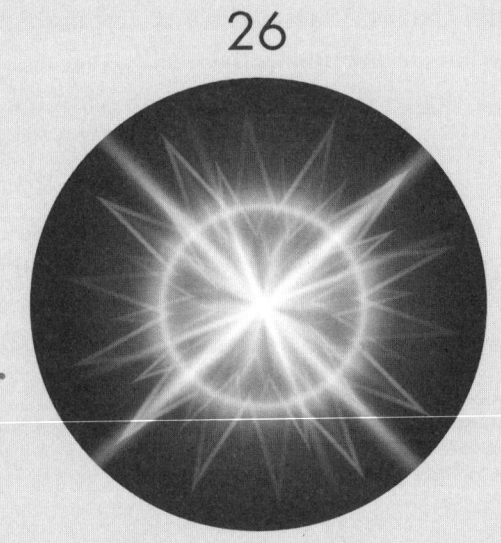

SELF-WORTH

No-one can make you feel inferior without your consent.

ELEANOR ROOSEVELT

*To have self-worth is to have moved beyond
the belief that valuing ourselves is egotistical.
It is a recognition that we are unique and loveable,
just as we are. Only when we have come to this
point can we really begin to manifest ourselves in
the world and take a full part in a relationship.*

You ARE WORTH A great deal, but you just don't seem to see that right now. Others, however, probably do, and will be drawn to exploit your good nature with ease.

You may see this exploitation as you giving love. But ask yourself whether it's not more a matter of needing to feel needed or to be worthy through someone else's eyes? A lack of self-worth tends to produce kindness or niceness to everybody except oneself.

It may be that your self-esteem is so low, you rarely put yourself in a position to even *have* a relationship. And if you do, you're so grateful for someone choosing to be with you, that your real self-expression goes out of the window for fear of driving the other person away.

But consider this: if you cannot value yourself just as you are, you will continue to attract partners who mirror this self-rejection – for the value you put on yourself is the value others put on you.

It may help to look back at your childhood and question where you received the message you were not good enough – perhaps not loveable. And then consider if you want to go on believing that. As long as you believe it and continue to put yourself down, others will, too. The world, in its cool, impassive fashion, will provide endless ways to prove you right!

In choosing this card today, you are asked to look at the wounded child within, who didn't receive the love he or she needed and is still looking to be validated from outside. You must find the wounded part and see what you can do to hold this child in love. Feel for yourself. Be kind to yourself. Parent yourself as you would have wanted to be parented then. If you try to manipulate your partner into giving you the reassurance or security you feel you lacked, then you will ultimately be disappointed. Your partner is *not* your parent.

Begin to see how power and control are being played out in your life. The fact is that the manipulations of your victim stance are based on the belief that you can't get power any other way. But in seeking to please and appease, you are just as guilty of trying to control your partner – into staying around or being nice to you – as someone who is blatantly dominating.

It really is time to stop trying to prove yourself and imagining that others are better than you. You are infinitely precious and truly amazing in your uniqueness. The moment you connect with that, your life will begin to change.

INVERSE

As long as we continue to measure our self-worth through the externals of life, we continue to lack self-worth.

IT SEEMS YOU ARE CONCEALING your innate sense of worthlessness behind a façade of superiority. Rather than valuing yourself, you are measuring your worth by your roles and your material success, or lack of it. You may have convinced many, including yourself, that this is who you are.

Whatever your social situation, the message is the same – stop identifying with the superficialities of life. Measuring yourself by where you live, who you know and what you and your partner look like could be enticing you away from the truth. Your real worth is in the essence of who you are.

This may be a hard message for you to accept, for you are being challenged for having an over-inflated ego. But over-inflation or 'acting big' is just another ploy to compensate for feeling small inside. The paradox is that as long as you go on believing it's the trappings of your life that make you special, you will never feel special and loved for yourself.

The issue you are dealing with now is demanding you to look beyond the superficialities of life, deeper inside than you may have ever done before. Once you can acknowledge the true worth of your own simple humanity, you will recognize the worth of others, too.

27

SEXUALITY

The sexual act is not for the depositing of seed. It is for the leaping off into the unknown, as from a cliff's edge ...

D. H. LAWRENCE

When our hearts and bodies meet and merge, the most powerful and intimate feeling becomes possible – union with another.

Your challenge is to allow the full expression of your sexuality in all its beauty and power.

When we are unsure of ourselves or want to stay in control, we make love with our mind and emotions more than with our body and our heart. Sexual experiences are often limited or, at best, unsatisfying 'fixes'. And our partners may become objectified – providing just a means of release – or perhaps someone to try to keep satisfied.

Are you scared of really letting go of your wildness? Scared of being overwhelmed or overwhelming – of being hurt? If you are holding yourself back sexually, the chances are that you are holding back your love as well.

You need to realize that being a good lover has nothing to do with 'doing it right' or looking good. It's all about staying connected and in touch with feeling. For the true expression of sexuality demands that the feelings of the heart are connected to the body – not the emotions and not the mind.

As well as this, it asks that you take responsibility for yourself and not for your partner. For, as long as you believe it is your task to satisfy your partner, you will be directing operations from your head.

You don't need a sex manual to be a wonderful lover! You and your partner have all the knowledge you need. And that knowledge is not in your heads; it's in your bodies. You need to take a leap of faith and recognize that in staying connected with your body and your heart, everything else will follow.

If you are feeling insecure about your sexuality, see if you are undermining your own confidence by bringing your beliefs and past experiences into the present. Start again. Behave as if you have never made love before and are about to begin on a whole new voyage of discovery. Let your body take the lead, and allow it to say 'No' or 'Yes' or 'More' when it wants to. Give yourself permission to take it slowly and, most important of all, if you want to stop at any point, stop!

The body is like a very sensitive child. If it feels it is unacceptable in some way, it won't act naturally. Instead, it will try to follow instructions from your mind, to do what it believes it's supposed to do, and often fail. But once given permission, the body can be a wonderfully expressive being – joyful, creative and deeply feeling.

Your body knows how and when to make love. Trust it. Let go of expectations and preconceptions of how things are supposed to be, and just stay with the present. It's far more important to enjoy each moment of the journey than to arrive at the destination.

Trust yourself, trust your body and open your heart – to yourself and your partner. All loving is a risk, but in allowing your vulnerability, you also tap into incredible power. Above all, don't be scared of showing your love!

INVERSE

When we use sexuality as a means of wielding power, it is abusive and ultimately damaging, both to ourselves and our sexual partners.

RATHER THAN ALLOWING your sexuality to be the sensitive and extraordinary expression of your feelings that it can be, you seem to be using it manipulatively, to seduce others or gratify yourself, without reference to the truth of your heart.

Such misuse serves to dull sensitivity and can lead either to unusual sexual practices in search of a greater high, or to an abandonment of love in favour of physical pleasure alone.

Maybe you think you can only be appreciated for your sexuality and are attracting partners who fulfil your belief. This will not change until *you* do. And the difficulty may be that you dare not be different, for fear of attracting no-one.

As with any other form of expression, sexuality needs to be contained – kept within certain boundaries

– and experienced appropriately. Over-investment in sexual pleasure means under-investment in the closer, deeper areas of a relationship.

Partners can offer more than temporary relief. Experiencing real closeness can heal. Sexuality can be an integral part of that process, if only you can risk allowing more of your vulnerability to show.

28

SPONTANEITY

Anyone who has never made a mistake has never tried anything.

ALBERT EINSTEIN

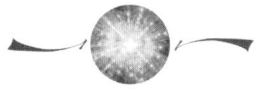

*Spontaneity is the impulsive, unpredictable action that adds zest to a relationship.
Passion is moments of spontaneity joined together.*

IT SEEMS IT'S TIME to just do it! Whatever you are faced with is demanding that you let go of rigidity, habit and your view of safety, and take a spontaneous dive into the unknown.

All too often we leave our spontaneous, adventurous sides back in childhood, perhaps because they were frowned upon by parents and other authority figures. But for you, now is the time to reclaim your spirit of adventure. And remember that, in a relationship, spontaneity is part of wildness and passion!

Without spontaneity, relationships can become lifeless and predictable. So, question yourself on how you are holding on to the familiar – staying within your comfort zone and following routines. Then wonder how this card applies to you.

Sometimes we just have to stop playing it safe and act, without pausing for thought and without knowing the outcome.

Someone once said: 'Life is not a rehearsal.' Are you living as if it is? What would happen if you stepped out of role and tried a new script, instead of repeating the same old scenes, over and over again?

Surprise someone! Shock yourself! Do something wild! Give yourself something to smile about when you're eighty!

INVERSE

A restless spirit often disguises a fear of commitment and intimacy.

WHAT YOU ARE PORTRAYING as spontaneity in fact may be a habit of creating things for yourself to do in order to avoid something.

Perhaps you are trying to make your partner out to be a stick-in-the-mud, while you paint yourself as a free spirit, ever ready to seek out new adventures.

Or perhaps you never really have a partner – just 'ships-in-the-night' relationships – because, once dawn breaks you're looking for the next ship; the next adventure on the horizon.

In either case, you are being asked to reflect on how this will-o'-the-wisp behaviour can ever lead to a real relationship.

Come into harbour, furl the sail and drop anchor. Spend some time getting to know who you and your partner are, without distractions.

In slowing down, you may face some discomfort, even some vulnerability, for that is what you've been avoiding. But you will also get to explore true intimacy.

29

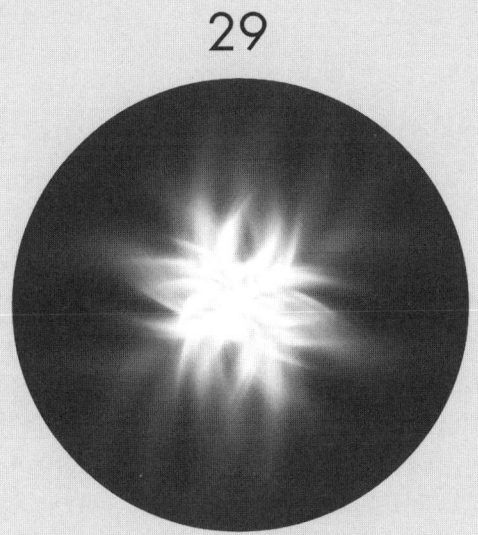

TRUST

*Faith is an oasis in the heart
which will never be reached by
the caravan of thinking.*

KAHLIL GIBRAN

Trust is having the confidence to be true to ourselves and to act without knowing the outcome.

YOU APPEAR TO BE SUFFERING from self-doubt – hesitating over a decision that you have made. Perhaps this decision is at odds with someone else and you fear a conflict, or perhaps you are just scared of being wrong.

Doubt usually arises when we're feeling challenged or threatened – when there's a steep mountain ahead of us and a lush, green valley behind, and we can't see past the mountain. We turn, look back, and wonder if the valley wasn't so bad after all.

That valley could be a behaviour pattern, a lifestyle, a way of relating, or a person. But what's familiar is not necessarily in our best interests.

Sometimes self-doubt arises when we make a decision that subsequently feels uncomfortable. We equate discomfort with being wrong and so begin to mistrust our decision and with it, ourselves. But the unfamiliar *can* feel uncomfortable. And there are occasions when we need to simply allow that discomfort and move into the unknown.

Sometimes a mountain needs to be climbed, just to see what's on the other side.

In drawing this card, you have clearly decided something that has set you on the path to the mountain. You are now faced with a choice: whether to continue on that path and go through with what you've set in motion, or to turn back. To trust yourself – or not.

Let go of the urge to think, and follow your heart's knowing. Trust and truth are twinned and you learn to trust by being true to yourself, to your inner-most feelings.

If you carry on climbing, the outcome may or may not be what you think you want. But it *will* be what you need.

INVERSE

When belief in ourselves means being deaf to others, self-trust has become defensiveness.

YOU ARE BEING ASKED to question whether the trust you have in your own beliefs and opinions is in fact defensiveness.

Trusting yourself doesn't necessarily mean being right. You can only trust as much as you know – which, of course, isn't everything. So self-trust has to be tempered with openness to being wrong and listening to others.

If this does not happen, over time narcissism can develop, where you believe only in yourself and spend a great deal of energy in proving how misguided and untrustworthy the rest of the world is – and manipulating people and situations to prove yourself right! And this very effectively keeps everyone, but most especially your partner, at bay.

Naturally, one of the problems with this way of being is the difficulty in seeing it, since you will tend to reject suggestions that you might be misguided.

And underlying all of this there may be a belief that you can't trust anyone anyway, exaggerating the need to rely on yourself.

The time has come to relax this self-reliance. How about starting by just wondering: 'What if?'

What if you *weren't* always right in your assumptions?

What if someone else *did* have something valuable to offer?

Would it be such a great risk to let someone touch you with their reality?

30

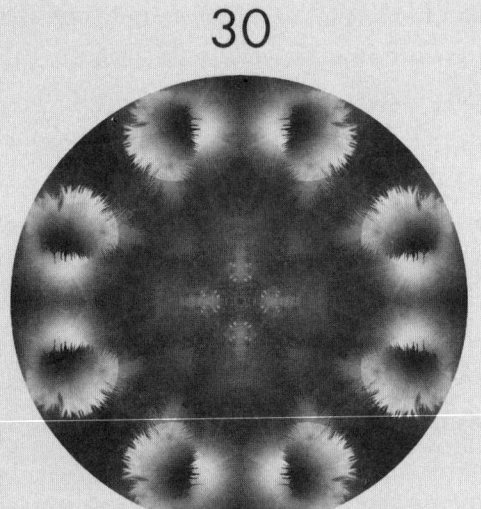

VULNERABILITY

*If we only ever reveal what we believe
to be acceptable, we can only
ever feel unacceptable.*

JOANNE L. HALL

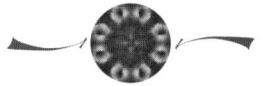

Vulnerability is having a very deep connection to our feelings and letting them show. When we are truly vulnerable no-one can doubt our honesty – for in our openness there is no manipulation or control.

YOU SEEM CONCERNED that you will get hurt if you express what you feel. So you are trying to control the situation by hiding the strength of your feelings, or even showing nothing.

You need to let go of this fear and show your feelings, without any expectations of how they will be received. Vulnerability only happens when you soften your whole being and drop your defences. All focus is then on the inner and there can be no concern for the outer, particularly for what people may think of you.

There are times when we must walk naked and defenceless, revealing our weaknesses as much as our strengths, our pain as much as our joy. We risk rejection – and we risk being loved more deeply.

Many people associate vulnerability with feeling exposed or letting themselves down. But in reality it is the false self, the mask you show to the world, that you're letting down. Concerns about being overwhelmed by feeling, or overwhelming another, may also be restricting you, but people are far less fragile than you think. The more you can expose your deepest feelings, the more connected you will feel – not only to your partner, but to *all* of life.

The extraordinary thing about vulnerability is that when we do allow ourselves to be seen in our nakedness, we emerge far stronger and more ready to express ourselves truthfully in the future, rather than feeling the weakness we most fear.

Risk saying: 'I'm sad'; 'I love you'; 'I'm hurting'; 'I miss you', if that's the truth. It might feel like you're heading down a dark corridor, not knowing where you'll end up. But your words will be like keys to rooms you never knew were there, unlocking the richness of the feelings you've been hiding away. For in the space of vulnerability lie the treasures of your heart.

INVERSE

Where vulnerability is open and seeks no reaction, self-pity is closed and hopes for rescue.

Perhaps you wonder how anyone can treat you so cold-heartedly, when you feel so bad. But isn't the way you're expressing yourself slightly manipulative?

Are you sulking, like a child, wanting others to make it better for you, or trying to blame someone else for your discomfort? Underneath your tears or protestations there is a deeper level of hurt, but you are fighting to deny it by accusing someone or something else.

There's a world of difference between genuine vulnerability and self-pity. In the latter, you seek to control people by playing vulnerable and eliciting sympathy. But it is not through other people that you will find healing.

Make the choice to stop acting the victim and reclaim your power. Recognize that you are being faced by the very real needs of a hurting inner child, but that it's time to look to your own adult side to provide the love and consideration that are so desperately needed.

31

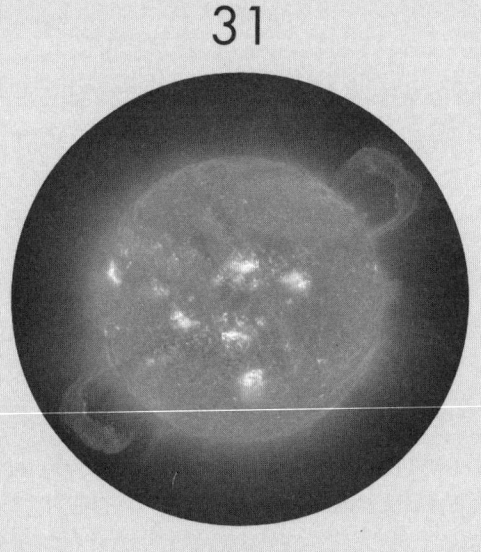

WILL

*Great souls have wills;
feeble ones have only wishes.*

CHINESE PROVERB

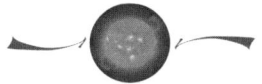

*Will harnesses intention and transforms it to action.
It is the resoluteness to carry on through,
no matter what.*

YOU ARE PROBABLY FEELING UNSURE of yourself. It may seem to you that there are obstacles in your path, causing you to both doubt your own strength and wonder whether your intention or goal is right.

When your willpower weakens, a mist descends and the way forward becomes unclear. Rather than carrying on, you may be frozen by doubt, fearful of plunging over an impending precipice. And your doubt continues to thicken the mist …

Take an objective look at the things that are trying to draw you away from your intention. They probably come from fear – of failing, of getting it wrong, of making yourself vulnerable. But consider this: they could be based on a fear of *success* and all that would mean to you!

Will clears a path through the mists of hesitancy and doubt.

To call on your will, focus on the goal rather than on all the things that might get in the way. The surest path to failure is to think about failing. The surest path to success is to believe that you will succeed.

Hold your goal in your mind and imagine it is already reality. That way, will kicks in, encouraging you forward, inspiring you with the persistence to achieve your purpose.

Of course, with any goal, there will always be fluctuations of energy and confidence. But the sooner you clarify your intention and boldly declare: 'This is what I want', the stronger you will feel.

INVERSE

When will dictates, there is no consideration for the other.

YOU MAY THINK that you are just being sensible by taking control and directing matters. But in fact, by following your own agenda and ignoring what is happening for someone else, you could be laying a minefield that you will ultimately have to cross. The crushed feelings of others do not go away, and in relationships they can be trodden on one time too many.

In thinking and acting as if you know best, you are not only manipulating your partner, but also hiding how scared you are of the gentler realms of receptivity, consideration and respect.

Recognize that there are two approaches to your relationship: beating into submission or partnering; fear or love.

Which do you really want?

32

THE MIRROR

Learning is finding out what you already know.

RICHARD BACH

The Mirror Card directs you back to yourself.

NOTHING IS REFLECTED HERE but the purity of your own inner knowing, and any search for understanding outside yourself would be a denial of that knowing.

Look into the mirror.

Accept that you *do* know all you need to know at this time.

FURTHER READING

The Art of Loving, Erich Fromm, Thorsons, 1995
The Eden Project: In Search of the Magical Other, James Hollis,
　　Inner City Books, 1998
Getting the Love you Want, Harville Hendrix, Pocket Books, 1993
Intimacy and Solitude: Balancing Closeness and Independence, Stephanie Dowrick,
　　The Women's Press, 2002
Journey of the Heart, John Welwood, HarperPerennial, 1996
The Politics of Experience, R.D. Laing, Penguin, 1990
The Psychology of Romantic Love, Robert A. Johnson, Arkana, 1984
Under Saturn's Shadow: The Wounding and Healing of Men, James Hollis,
　　Inner City Books, 1994
What Life Should Mean to You, Alfred Adler, George Allen, 1980

AUTHORS' ACKNOWLEDGEMENTS

The authors are grateful to the copyright holders below for permission to reproduce the following text extracts:

p.28, *Cittaviveka*, Ajahn Sumedho, ©Amaravati Publications, 1992;
p.38 & p.89, *Gayan*, Inayat Khan, Omega Publications, 1988; p.79, *Who Dies?*,
Stephen Levine, ©Anchor Books, 1982; p.112, *How Does it Feel?*, Mick Csaky,
©Thames & Hudson, 1979; p.141, *The Prophet*, Kahlil Gibran,
William Heinemann, 1980; p.161, *Sand and Foam*, Kahlil Gibran,
©Alfred Knopf, 1954; p.174, *Illusions*, Richard Bach, Pan, 1978.

Every effort has been made to contact copyright holders. In those cases where this has proved difficult we apologise and request that the copyright holder contact us via the publisher.

With warmest thanks to: Robert Kirby and Connie Dunne-Kirby for mirroring our belief; Oliver Burston for his powerful reflections of the text; and all at Eddison Sadd for turning the mirror to the world.

EDDISON • SADD EDITIONS

EDITORIAL DIRECTOR: Ian Jackson	ART DIRECTOR: Elaine Partington
EDITOR: Katie Ginn	PROJECT DESIGNER: Malcolm Smythe
PROOFREADER: Peter Kirkham	PRODUCTION: Oonagh Phelan and Charles James